'These lovely boys always
create incredibly tasty food'
JAMIE OLIVER

'Proper good food . . . hearty, decent and delicious'
RUSSELL BRAND

'The poster boys for a healthy way of life!'
SUNDAY TIMES

'Their energy is almost tangible'
DR RANGAN CHATTERJEE

'A healthy-eating phenomenon'
MAIL ON SUNDAY

'The boys are helping to make the world
a healthier, happier place . . . what's not to love?'
VEGAN FOOD AND LIVING

'Great people, unbelievable food'
JOE WICKS

DAVID & STEPHEN FLYNN

THE HAPPY PEAR

VEGAN

cooking for

everyone

ESSENTIAL TIPS AND TECHNIQUES FOR

DELICIOUS PLANT-BASED COOKING

Photography by Alistair Richardson

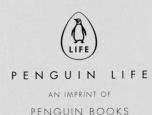

PENGUIN LIFE

AN IMPRINT OF

PENGUIN BOOKS

CONTENTS

INTRODUCTION

Would you love to cook more but don't know where to start?

Do you like cooking but feel lost without a recipe, envious of people who can conjure a meal out of a handful of bits and pieces from their store cupboard?

Or having heard so much talk about the benefits of plant-based eating – both for health and for the planet – would you like to eat more veg? Or are you already vegetarian or vegan but need some inspiration?

Well, you are holding the answer to all these questions – welcome to *Vegan Cooking for Everyone*!

This is our biggest ever cookbook, with nearly 250 recipes, but more than that, we will walk you through the basics of how dishes are created so that even when you don't have a recipe you will have no problem creating a meal. Everything you need to know is broken down into its essential elements and explained clearly.

We never thought we would become competent vegan chefs. But after cooking in our own café and restaurant kitchens for over a decade, having written three bestselling cookbooks and having our recipes viewed 20 million times online, we understand what is essential (and what is not) and have done our best to distil our knowledge into this book.

We believe that understanding how ingredients come together and getting to grips with some simple techniques will give you freedom and confidence in your kitchen. You can still continue to use cookbooks (we hope you do!), but you'll be able to adapt recipes to suit yourself and you won't need a cookbook to create great dishes. Keep reading and we will teach you how to cook exceptional vegan food.

* * *

'Vegan' used to be a divisive word. When we changed from being stereotypical meat-eating, beer-drinking jocks to eating a plant-based diet nearly 20 years ago, most people thought we had lost the plot. We had discovered vegan eating separately on our travels after college and it just felt right for both of us, and we've never looked back. We knew we felt great and the more we looked into it, the more we understood the health benefits of our new way of eating.

Following a plant-based diet also made us realize that food isn't just about our next meal, but that what we eat affects the environment, the climate and the economy. It gave us a sense of connection with our community and the planet as a whole.

We used to seem like way-out idealists talking about all this, but this thinking is becoming increasingly mainstream. Plant-based eating is no longer seen as a fad, but is about making a positive choice. And you don't have to go totally vegan to make that choice – just mixing up your diet and having more plant-based meals is good for your wallet, your waistline and the world.

So when we say 'for everyone' in the title of this book, we really mean it – the more the merrier. If you're just dipping your toe into vegan waters, come on in! The book has lots of simple and delicious vegan recipes that will become new favourites. And you can also start to experiment and explore possibilities you might never have imagined. With *Vegan Cooking for Everyone* as your guide, you will discover an approach to cooking that will liberate and inspire you. We would go so far as to say that this book could revolutionize your life!

HOW TO USE THIS BOOK

We've done things differently in this book. First, we have included a certain amount of key information at the start of each chapter before you get stuck into the cooking. Second, we haven't presented the recipes in the traditional format – ingredients, method and a picture. Instead, we have put the recipes into handy frameworks. Each framework gives you multiple sets of ingredients, arranged in columns, and these all follow the same cooking instructions – so with each framework you are getting up to five recipes for the price of one!

For simplicity, each framework comes after we set out the shared step-by-step method for making the recipes it includes – so you'll understand how everything comes together before you decide which variation you want to try first. For example, our wholefood burgers framework (p. 127) includes three recipes – High-Protein Burger, Basic Burger and 15-Minute Burger – and the common method of making all three is on p. 126.

By presenting the recipes this way, we want to demystify them and to show you that apparently different recipes have common elements. Once you see and understand how recipes are structured you'll be liberated – you can follow our recipes, vary them or even come up with your own!

But before we get to the recipes, first let's talk about the foundations of all good food, not just vegan cooking: the five basic flavours and how to balance them, flavour agents and seasoning, texture and garnishes. Once you've got a handle on all that, you can fearlessly dive into the cooking.

THE FIVE BASIC FLAVOURS AND HOW TO BALANCE THEM

There are five 'tastes' that are the foundation of the flavours in every recipe: salty, bitter, sweet, sour/acid and umami. Some tastes can be stronger in certain dishes than others, but making the perfect dish is all about balancing these flavours and creating harmony.

1. Salty

Salt has the greatest capacity to add flavour of any of the five elements. Salt minimizes bitterness, balances sweetness, develops aromas and unlocks flavours. When a recipe says 'season to taste', this generally refers to adding salt until the dish tastes balanced. If you haven't added enough salt no amount of fancy cooking techniques will make up for it, so learning to season properly with salt is one of the most essential aspects of good cooking.

This doesn't mean that you need to add more salt to your food, but rather, that you should use salt better. Salt breaks down the external cell walls in fruit and veg and allows flavours to marry together, which is why you should add it while boiling, sweating or frying veg or cooking grains, so you season them from the inside and not just at the end of the cooking time before serving. It also creates and accentuates the contrast between flavours, such as the differences between sweet and sour.

When food tastes flat and bland the most common problem is a lack of salt, so try adding a little more salt before you look to the other elements of flavour. Take a spoonful of the dish, sprinkle it with a tiny amount of salt, taste it and see if that makes the dish taste better. If it does, season the whole dish by adding more salt.

Knowing how much salt to add to achieve harmony can be a subtle balance. Always start with just a little, adding a small amount at a time – you can always add more, but you can't take it out if you add too much. Sometimes dishes need only the slightest pinch of salt to make them taste balanced and perfect. Seasoning is an incremental process and the most important thing is to taste, taste and then taste some more.

Keep in mind, too, that all salt is not made equally. We use two main types of salt: fine sea salt and flaky sea salt. Fine sea salt is used for everyday – we use it for most of our cooking. Flaky sea salt, such as Maldon, is generally more expensive than fine salt, as it takes longer to produce. It's used for finishing dishes, as it adds a lovely flaky texture. We use it to finish roasted veg, toasties, stews, pastas, pizzas – just about anything, really. One tablespoon of flaky sea salt will be two to three times less salty than 1 tablespoon of fine sea salt, as the fine salt will compact more in the spoon than the bigger crystals of flaky salt.

In our recipes, when we refer to salt we always mean fine sea salt, as this is what is used in most cooking. There are also other varieties of salt with their own distinctive flavour, such as kala namak or black sulphur salt, which tastes of sulphur or almost like eggy salt – we use this to create an egg flavour in vegan scrambled eggs or omelettes (see p. 51). Other types of salts include seaweed salts, with a note of the sea, and truffle salts to give that fancy earthy truffle note.

A salty flavour can be obtained from other sources too. Seaweed, such as dulse or kombu, can be added to the base of stews or you can season a dish with dried seaweed, which also adds more minerals to the dish. A few olives or capers also make a great salty addition to a dish – capers are like little salty bombs with a nice acidity to them too.

2. Bitter

We don't eat much bitter food nowadays, as it's become a less desirable taste. However, bitter food is generally very beneficial for our digestion and overall health, as many sources of the bitter flavour are green leafy vegetables, such as kale, spinach, chicory and endives. Other bitter foods include veg such as broccoli, cauliflower and artichokes, fruits such as grapefruit, lemon, lime and orange, and grains such as millet and amaranth.

A few years back, we were travelling in Italy and were amazed at how bitter greens are still part of the daily diet there, from chicory and broccoli rabe to dente di leone (dandelion greens). Italians eat these greens as a side dish, in pasta and even in sandwiches. Although bitterness sounds like an undesirable flavour to many people, it widens the palette of flavours in a dish and heightens the contrast. Try adding some baby spinach or chopped kale to finish a dish, as it ups the nutritional profile, adds more colour and creates more flavour contrast by adding a bitter note that will heighten and accentuate the sweet notes.

The quickest way to balance a bitter taste is with salt rather than a sweetener. If a dish tastes too bitter, start by adding a little salt and see how that affects the taste before adding a sweetener.

3. Sweet

This is the flavour that many of us love the most! Sweet is biologically desirable, as traditionally it indicated that fruits were ripe and their sugars or calories were more available and easier to digest. As a result, a sweet taste signals our brains to release dopamine, our pleasure hormone, which relaxes us and gives us a nice feeling. It also tells us to eat more.

A lot of people get caught up with the question of what the best sweetener is, but it's important to remember that most sweeteners – even natural ones such as maple, agave or date syrup – are refined. This means that the fibre has been removed from a fruit or vegetable, extracting nothing but the liquid sweetness, which tastes great but isn't great for our health. The less refined sweeteners you eat, the better, but we do love a good dessert or sweet treat every now and then. The ideal sweeteners in terms of health are ones made from wholefood sources such as dates or other dried fruit, as these still have their fibre.

Most fresh fruits and vegetables such as sweet potatoes, carrots, onions, squashes and parsnips are naturally sweet. Cinnamon is a spice that has a warming sweetness to it.

To use sweetness to balance a dish we try to use dried fruit, but if that won't work we'll add a little maple syrup. The combination of sweet and salty in a dish is a hugely popular contrast.

4. Sour/acid

Acid is indispensable to everything we cook. Even the smallest addition of a sour ingredient, such as a squeeze of lime or a splash of apple cider vinegar, can really brighten up a dish. We love to add a squeeze of lemon or lime to all our curries, as we find it gives the dish a final kick of flavour.

Anything with a pH below 7 is sour or acidic. Acid in its pure sense is sour, but there are many different sources of acid, such as coffee, Earl Grey tea, ketchup, tomatoes and vinegar. Some other sour foods include sourdough bread, wheat, sauerkraut and citrus fruit.

Salty, fatty, bitter and starchy foods all benefit from acid, as it creates more contrast. For example, in guacamole the lime will cut through the fat to give a whole other dimension of flavour and lightness to the dish.

There are three main ways of developing an acid note in foods. The first is browning your veg, which will create more complex flavours (including acid) and will also add more sweetness due to the caramelization. The other methods are fermentation and pickling (see p. 307 for some quick pickle recipes).

Acid dulls green leaves, such as salad, so add it just before serving. However, it can accentuate pink and red colours, such as pickled red onions, making the colour really pop. Some raw fruits and veg oxidize once they've been cut, but acid will help to stop this. Try squeezing a drop of lemon on chopped apples, globe artichokes or avocados to stop them browning.

Acid is like the opposite of salt – while salt heightens flavour, acid balances it. It's obvious when a food is too salty, but acid is a lot more subjective and relative. Some of us love acid, while others are a lot more sensitive to it.

Acidity is balanced by sweetness. When using acid as a seasoning, consider layering the acid as you cook and remember that a little goes a long way when it comes to sourness. For example, when making a tomato sauce, which is acidic, consider adding a splash of red wine vinegar or balsamic vinegar to accentuate this acid note, then adding some grated carrot or a liquid sweetener to balance the acidity. The most basic thing to say about the addition of acid (which is also central to most seasoning) is to taste as you go and trust your instincts as to what tastes good to you.

5. Umami

While it is similar in flavour to saltiness, umami also adds that final note to a dish. Umami wasn't recognized as a flavour in Western culture until 1985, but it has been an important part of Asian cuisine since the early 1900s. The nearest translation in English is 'deliciousness' or 'savouriness'. It is the result of a flavour compound called glutamates, the most well-known of which is monosodium glutamate (MSG), a white powder often used in Chinese restaurants to enhance flavour. However, it also occurs naturally in food such as ripe tomatoes, tomato concentrate, tomato ketchup, mushrooms, yeast products such as nutritional yeast and Marmite, and fermented foods such as tamari, soy sauce and miso.

The quintessential umami foods that we use are tamari (a wheat-free soy sauce), soy sauce and miso. These are all fermented and traditionally take years to make, so they are a concentrated source of flavour that also really packs that umami punch like few other foods can.

When adding umami to balance a dish, always add it along with salt and acid to heighten the flavour without having to do much work. When we have to dilute soups or stews if they're too thick, the first thing we use to add instant flavour is tamari, as it immediately adds more depth and more saltiness without adding salt.

FLAVOUR AGENTS AND SEASONING

The most important tool when seasoning and playing with flavour is your own palate. Taste, taste and taste again. It's important that you season and taste your dish as you cook each element rather than leaving it all to the end, as that way you will ensure you have developed flavour all the way through the cooking process.

Salt: As mentioned above, salt is one of the main ways to accentuate flavour. When seasoning, always start with a little salt at a time and try to achieve a balanced harmony to suit your tastes.

Tamari or soy sauce: Tamari is a wheat-free soy sauce that is aged in oak barrels and usually comes from Japan. It adds a moreish umami element. Make sure to add tamari or soy sauce in proportion to salt, as both contain sodium and it's easy to overdo the salty taste if you use both. Start by adding a little tamari or soy sauce at a time, taste and keep adjusting accordingly. If you overdo the sodium, you'll have to adjust your dish by adding more starch/beans or unseasoned sauce to try to distribute the sodium more evenly.

Lemon/lime: The juice of half a lemon or a whole lime will add a fresh citrus sharpness to a dish. Use either lemon or lime or a capful of vinegar (such as apple cider or rice vinegar), but not both, as they serve the same purpose – these are all acids, which help to cut through starch or fat and enliven food that can otherwise seem flat and dull. Acid is best added at the end of the cooking time, just before serving, as cooking can cause acid to lose its vibrancy.

Vinegars: Whether it's a red or white wine vinegar, apple cider vinegar, rice vinegar or mirin (a Japanese wine vinegar), it all adds acid to a dish. We use vinegar to balance out and cut through a 'tight', heavy dish.

Fresh herbs: We use the more delicate fresh herbs, such as coriander, parsley, chives and basil, as a garnish to finish a dish right before serving, as they usually lose their flavour during the heat of cooking. However, hardier herbs such as thyme, rosemary and bay leaf are added during cooking.

Spices: Spices will add more flavour and depth to your dish. In our cafés we have a huge variety of spices that we're always adding to, but at home you can get by with 10 to 15 core spices. Spices tend to be reasonably cheap and will last a long time if kept sealed and stored in a cool, dark place.

Here are the spices we use the most and the type of dishes we use them in. The main thing to keep in mind when it comes to spices and seasoning is to start by adding a small amount to your dish and taste it, then add a little more if you think it needs it, until you reach your desired taste.

- Ground cumin: Quite a forgiving spice, as it's aromatic rather than spicy, so you can add a couple of teaspoons per 500ml of sauce without it massively affecting a dish (unlike chilli powder!). This robust spice is great in curries, Moroccan dishes and Mexican food.

- Whole cumin seeds: These add a bit of texture. We toast them in a hot, dry pan for 5 minutes or so, until they start to pop, to release their flavour. We will typically add 1 tablespoon per 500ml of sauce. Like ground cumin, the whole seeds are great in curries, Moroccan dishes and Mexican food. Ground cumin will disperse evenly throughout a dish, while cumin seeds will end up in some mouthfuls and not others and will give a pop of flavour and a nice bite.

- Ground coriander: An aromatic spice that is more forgiving than the likes of chilli powder, so we tend to use it quite generously in curries, Moroccan dishes and Mexican food.

- Coriander seeds: We toast these in a hot, dry pan for 5 minutes or so, until they start to pop, then grind them using a pestle and mortar or a high-speed blender. We nearly always use them if we're also using cumin seeds. We typically add 1 tablespoon (ground) per 500ml of sauce.

- Ground turmeric: Quite bitter or astringent and has a very dry taste. We typically limit turmeric to 1 teaspoon per 800ml of sauce. It will make the dish turn yellow or give it a yellow-brown hue. We use it in many of our curries.

- **Curry powder (medium):** As the name implies, it goes great in all curries! We usually use 1 to 2 tablespoons per 800ml of sauce.

- **Ground cinnamon:** Adds a distinct aromatic flavour to dishes and a sweet, woody fragrance. We use cinnamon when we are cooking something with Moroccan flavours or an Indian or Sri Lankan curry.

- **Ground black pepper:** Black pepper is ground from dried, whole, unripe fruit. It adds a musky spice to dishes and is often used in tandem with salt. You can use ground black pepper or grind your own peppercorns. It's a strong spice, so we limit it to ½ teaspoon per 500ml of sauce.

- **Paprika (sweet):** When a recipe simply calls for paprika, it's referring to sweet paprika, which is fruity and a little bitter. It typically adds a vibrant, bright red colour to a dish. We sometimes sprinkle it over hummus as a garnish. It goes well in tomato-based dishes such as chilli or tagines and it's also great in curries.

- **Smoked paprika:** Smoked paprika uses peppers that are smoked and dried, then crushed to a powder. It has a distinct, almost meaty taste to it and gives a smoky note to dishes. It's very strong, so we use it sparingly, but if you like a strong smoky taste, you will love this spice.

- **Ground ginger:** Half spicy and peppery, half lemony, slightly sweet but pungent – that's how you might describe the flavour of ginger. It adds a lovely warmth and sharpness to dishes. Ground ginger can often taste more aromatic than fresh ginger.

- **Chilli powder (medium):** Chilli powder is usually a blend of a few spices used in Latin American cooking. It adds heat to dishes and a depth of flavour too. Omit chilli powder if you don't like heat, but if you do, start with a pinch at first and adjust accordingly.

- **Chilli flakes:** These are dried crushed chillies that contain the flesh and seeds of whole chillies. We typically use them as a garnish. Chilli flakes really spice up a meal and we use them in a range of dishes, from Italian and Indian, to Tex-Mex and Mexican.

TEXTURE

Good food appeals to all our senses. The appearance, smell and taste of a dish all play a part in our enjoyment of it. When it comes to preparing a meal that will deliver on all levels, it's also worth considering the textures of the different elements of your dish.

Contrast is really important in food and it's also true for texture. Having some gentle parts of a dish and some strong flavoured, some crunchy or crisp elements, some saucy and some dry, all helps to create harmony. Let's look at each element and how you can add it to your dish.

Crunch

A sprinkle of toasted seeds can work on a sweeter dish, such as porridge, or any savoury dish, such as a salad or soup. We love pumpkin seeds, sunflower seeds and sesame seeds. Toast your seeds in the oven or in a hot dry pan for a few minutes to add an extra depth of flavour.

A handful of raw or toasted nuts scattered over a dish adds a contrast of texture.

Tear stale bread into chunks and drizzle with a little oil, season with salt and some dried herbs, such as thyme and rosemary, and bake in the oven at 180°C fan/400°F/ gas 6 for 10 minutes, until crisp, to make simple croutons to add a nice crunch to salads and soups.

A pinch of a seed mix such as gomashio, dukkah or za'atar (see p. 310) adds a gentle crunch and a pop of flavour to salads, soups, stews and most savoury dishes.

Granola (see p. 31) is the perfect sweet and crunchy topping for all breakfast dishes. We love to sprinkle it on top of porridge, chia puddings and overnight oats.

Moisture

Coconut-based sauces add a fatty, moreish element to a dish. Using a tin of coconut milk as the base of a soup or curry sauce gives a dish a comforting richness.

Tomato-based sauces can deliver an element of sweetness or spiciness depending on what you add to them. They are great with pasta or as a base to a curry dish.

Salad dressings help to add moisture and flavour to a dry salad. Your base can be oil (olive oil is a good one for a neutral flavour), a dairy-free yoghurt for a creamier dressing or a fruit juice such as apple for an oil-free dressing.

Salsas are a great addition to many dishes as they bring an element of moisture. Try a simple tomato salsa made with chopped fresh tomatoes, a squeeze of lime juice, garlic, herbs, spices and seasoning.

Creaminess

When it comes to sauces, creaminess generally refers to a sauce having a nice mouthfeel from the fat contained in it. In vegan cooking we base our creamy sauces on coconut milk (see p. 202), an olive oil and pasta water emulsion (see p. 168), béchamel sauce (see p. 175), creamy cashew sauce (see p. 177) or a pesto-infused tomato sauce (see p. 152).

- Avocados are a great way of adding some creamy fattiness to a dish. Mashed on top of crunchy toast, wholegrain crackers or rice cakes, these beauties are super versatile.

- Hummus, pesto and tapenade (see pp. 312, 165, 318) are perfect for adding some creaminess to a dish. Foods such as dry sandwiches, falafel and crackers all come to life when paired with a tasty hummus or pesto.

- Nut and seed butters are a delicious addition to sweet and savoury meals. We love a dollop of almond butter on porridge or served with crunchy apple slices or banana. Almond butter, peanut butter and tahini are all great ways of adding a creamy richness to a dish, and a spoonful of them in a curry sauce can take it to next-level comfort food heaven!

- To add more creaminess to a sauce you can either add some cashew cream sauce (see p. 177), make a roux and add it to thicken (see p. 175), or add a little oil and ensure there is a starch that it can emulsify with.

Bite

Wholegrains such as brown rice and quinoa add a delicious bite to any savoury meal. Here are some of our favourite grains that can be paired with any savoury dish. All these grains can be eaten hot or cold in a salad.

- Brown rice: Has more bite and texture to it than white rice, as the whole grain is intact. Brown basmati rice has a slightly softer texture, while short-grain brown rice has a denser consistency and keeps its bite when cooked.

- Quinoa: Has a bead-like structure and when cooked has a light texture while retaining a good bite. Works well in hot dishes and salads. It's a pseudo grain, as it's actually a seed, so it's gluten free.

- Wholemeal couscous: The smallest of the three grains here, this is also the softest in texture and cooks in just a few minutes. It goes great with tagines and in flatbreads.

- Millet: Gentle, like a soft couscous, which is heralded for its digestive soothing properties. It is also gluten free.

GARNISHES

We eat with our eyes first, so a good garnish can make the difference between a dish presenting really well or looking very ordinary. Here is a list of some of the garnishes we use most often:

- Toasted flaked almonds (see p. 301)
- Toasted pumpkin and sunflower seeds (see p. 301)
- Sesame seeds
- Chilli flakes
- Finely chopped fresh herbs
- Crushed pink peppercorns
- Pomegranate seeds
- Chopped or crumbled nuts
- Lemon or lime wedges
- Desiccated coconut or coconut flakes
- Pickled veg (see p. 307)
- Gomashio, dukkah or za'atar seed mixes (see p. 310)

Breakfast

We love breakfast so much that we'd go so far as to say it's our favourite meal of the day. Breakfast can often be a routine meal that you make on autopilot, particularly during the week, when you might have the same thing every morning, but there is so much variety and so many options out there. We want to challenge you to try something different and push your boundaries, whether it's overnight oats or a chia pudding that you can make ahead of time, homemade granola, pancakes or a vegan fry at the weekend, complete with scrambled eggs, bacon, sausage, baked beans and greens.

OVERNIGHT OATS AND CHIA PUDDINGS

Overnight oats (also known as Bircher muesli) and chia puddings are super convenient and easy brekkies to make ahead of time so that you can have a batch ready in the fridge each morning when you wake up, then simply choose a different topping each day to keep things interesting. The more different-coloured fruits you use, the more vibrant it will look. We love kiwis, berries and bananas, to name just a few. Both the oats and the chia puddings are eaten cold, so they're great for summertime or in warm weather.

There is no end to the number of variations you can make, but there are a few essential components that are common to both that will give you the access code to chia pudding and overnight oat nirvana!

THE ESSENTIALS

Oats or chia seeds: Use whatever oats you have – regular porridge oats, jumbo oats and gluten-free oats will all work well. Chia seeds are packed with nutrition, so they're a great addition to your diet. You can get them in most supermarkets and health food stores these days. They swell up and form a pudding-like texture once soaked. You can soak them overnight or for 10 to 20 minutes before eating.

Liquid: You can use any non-dairy milk (sweetened or unsweetened) that you like or have in your fridge, a fruit juice, such as apple or orange juice, or even just water. You can also mix some non-dairy yoghurt, such as coconut or soya yoghurt, into your liquid for added creaminess. When making chia pudding, the basic ratio is one part chia seeds to six parts liquid.

Fruit: This is where you can really get creative. Fresh berries, chopped banana, kiwi or mango, halved grapes – go wild! The greater variety of fruit and the brighter the colours, the more impressive your dish will look and taste.

Optional extras: Here are a few optional extras that you could include directly in the mix or as toppings:

- 2 tablespoons chopped nuts
- 2 tablespoons desiccated coconut
- 2 tablespoons nut butter
- 1 tablespoon maple syrup or other sweetener
- ½ teaspoon cocoa powder
- ¼ teaspoon vanilla extract
- ¼ teaspoon ground cinnamon

How to serve: Our favourite way to serve overnight oats and chia puddings is to layer them with fruit compote (see p. 26) and coconut yoghurt in a clear glass or shallow bowl, like creating a triple-layer sundae! In a large glass or sundae dish, put the oat or chia mixture on the bottom, then add a layer of a colourful fruit compote, such as mango or berry, in the middle, then a good dollop of coconut yoghurt. Top with some granola, fresh fruit or cacao nibs to add extra flavour and crunch.

OVERNIGHT OATS

Serves 1 to 2

To make any of the overnight oat recipes gluten free, simply use gluten-free oats.

1. Mix all the ingredients together in a large bowl. You can either leave the entire batch in the bowl and cover it, or you can divide it between individual sealed jars.

2. Set aside to soak for 30 minutes or in the fridge overnight. You can make a batch up to 5 days in advance.

3. See the note above on our favourite way to serve overnight oats.

RECIPE:	BASIC OVERNIGHT OATS	BERRY OVERNIGHT OATS	MANGO AND CARDAMOM OVERNIGHT OATS
OATS	125g oats	50g oats	50g oats
CHIA SEEDS		25g chia seeds	25g chia seeds
NUTS OR SEEDS	20g pumpkin seeds	20g flaked almonds	30g mixed seeds
DRIED FRUIT	20g raisins	30g pitted dates, finely chopped	20g dried mango, finely chopped
LIQUID	300ml oat milk	300ml apple juice	300ml rice milk
FLAVOUR AGENTS	Pinch of ground cinnamon	50g fruit compote (p. 26)	Pinch of ground cardamom

BREAKDOWN ↑↓

CHIA PUDDING

Serves 1 to 2

1. Mix all the ingredients except the toppings together in a large bowl and whisk until all the chia seeds are submerged – if they aren't, you will have some crunchy ones, which will create a difference in texture. (If you're making the creamy, nutty chia pudding, first put the almond butter and non-dairy milk into a large bowl and whisk until smooth before adding all the other ingredients.)

2. Set aside to soak for 10 to 20 minutes or in the fridge overnight, until the pudding has become firm.

3. Before serving, use a fork to whisk the pudding to break it up and create a more homogeneous texture. If it's too thick, you may need to add an extra splash of non-dairy milk and whisk it through to loosen it to the right consistency. Or, if it's too runny, add 1 or 2 teaspoons of chia seeds and allow to sit for a further 10 minutes to thicken it.

4. You can make a batch up to 5 days in advance. See the note on p. 22 on our favourite way to serve chia pudding, or add any or all of the optional toppings listed in the framework.

RECIPE:	BASIC CHIA PUDDING	CREAMY COCONUT AND CINNAMON CHIA PUDDING	BERRY BURST CHIA PUDDING	CREAMY, NUTTY CHIA PUDDING
CHIA SEEDS	40g chia seeds	40g chia seeds	40g chia seeds	40g chia seeds
OATS			2 tbsp oats	
FRUIT			125g fresh or frozen raspberries	
SWEETENER	1½ tbsp maple syrup	1½ tbsp maple syrup	1 banana, mashed 1½ tbsp maple syrup	1½ tbsp maple syrup
FLAVOUR AGENTS	½ tsp ground cinnamon	½ tsp ground cinnamon		1 tsp raw cacao powder ½ tsp ground cinnamon
NON-DAIRY MILK OR YOGHURT	300ml rice milk	150g coconut yoghurt 200ml coconut or non-dairy milk	300ml rice milk	35g almond butter 250ml rice or almond milk
TOPPINGS (OPTIONAL)		Yoghurt Fresh fruit Granola (p. 31) Cacao nibs Seeds Goji berries Fruit compote (p. 26)	Yoghurt Fresh fruit Granola (p. 31) Cacao nibs Seeds Goji berries Fruit compote (p. 26)	Yoghurt Fresh fruit Granola (p. 31) Cacao nibs Seeds Goji berries Fruit compote (p. 26)

BREAKDOWN ↑ ↓

FRUIT COMPOTE AND STEWED FRUIT

Makes approx. 500g

We use fruit compote and stewed fruit to elevate porridge, overnight oats and chia puddings and they work great in a bowl of granola with yoghurt, on top of pancakes or in desserts.

Here is a framework for four of our favourite compotes and stewed fruits. We always use frozen fruit where possible, as it's cheaper and more convenient than using fresh fruit. We don't like our compotes to be too sweet and generally just rely on the natural sweetness of the fruit, but in the case of the rhubarb or Bramley apples, which can be a bit sour, you may want to use some sweetener.

1. Peel and core your fruit and chop into bite-size pieces if it needs it (we prefer to leave the skin on apples when making stewed apples).

2. Put the prepared fruit, water, sweetener and spice (if using) in a saucepan. If you're using cooking apples such as Bramleys in the stewed apples, you will have to add more sweetener.

3. Bring to the boil, then reduce the heat, put the lid on the pan and simmer gently for 20 minutes, stirring occasionally and checking to make sure there is enough water. The keys to stewing fruit are to make sure you have enough water in the pan so that the fruit doesn't burn and to keep the lid on to maintain the moisture, so add an extra splash of water if it's catching on the bottom of the pan.

4. When the fruit has broken down and is completely tender, we prefer to leave our compotes chunky, but if you prefer yours smooth, simply blend with a hand-held blender. These will all keep for up to 1 week in an airtight container in the fridge.

RECIPE:	STEWED APPLES	BERRY COMPOTE	RHUBARB, BANANA AND GINGER COMPOTE	MANGO PURÉE
FRUIT	500g apples	600g frozen berries	500g rhubarb 1 ripe banana	500g frozen mango
WATER	75ml water	50ml water	75ml water	50ml water
SWEETENER	2 tbsp maple syrup		3 tbsp maple syrup	
SPICE	Pinch of ground cinnamon (optional)	Pinch of ground cinnamon (optional)	½ tsp ground ginger	

BREAKDOWN ↑ ↓

GRANOLA

Granola is a crunchy breakfast cereal made with rolled oats, nuts, seeds, some form of fat, a sweetener and dried fruit. The main difference between granola and muesli is that granola is baked until it's crisp, toasted and golden brown, whereas muesli is left raw. Muesli generally doesn't have any sweetener or fat added to it either, but granola needs both of these to encourage the crispness, golden colour and caramelization when it's baked in the oven.

Granola is something else we make tonnes of every week, as we sell three types of granola in hundreds of supermarkets across Ireland. It's really straightforward once you understand the basic breakdown.

Sweetener: 10%

Oil: 10%

Dried fruit: 10%

Seeds: 10%

Nuts: 10%

Oats: 50%

THE ESSENTIALS

Oats: There are three main types of oats that you can use in granola:

- **Regular oat flakes:** These are the most readily available and work great, but they can sometimes be a bit powdery and they don't hold their structure as well as jumbo flakes when baked.

- **Jumbo oat flakes:** This is what we typically use, as they hold their shape the best. They don't go powdery and the granola doesn't clump together as much.

- **Gluten-free oat flakes:** If you are gluten intolerant or coeliac, then these are the best choice for you. They tend to come only in a standard-sized oat flake.

Nuts: Use whatever nuts you like or have on hand. You can add them whole or chop them up, depending on your preference. If you chop the nuts they will go further throughout the granola, which means you'll get more bang for your buck.

Seeds: The seeds we use most often are pumpkin, sunflower, sesame and chia, but again, use what you like or have on hand. Pumpkin seeds add a nice fleck of green and become a bit crunchier than the others due to their larger size.

Sweetener: Our framework uses a liquid sweetener rather than a granulated sugar, such as caster sugar. We tend to go with maple syrup, but you could use date syrup, brown rice syrup, agave syrup, apple syrup, coconut nectar, or whatever liquid sweetener you have or like best.

Oil: We use oil that doesn't have a strong flavour, as the purpose of the oil in granola is not to add flavour, but to ensure that the oats crisp up nicely when baked. We use a medium-grade sunflower oil the most, as it has a neutral flavour. If you use a high-grade oil, such as cold-pressed sunflower or olive oil, it will have a strong, distinct flavour that will overpower the taste of your granola, so it's best to avoid them. We also use coconut oil sometimes, which gives a crisp texture with a subtle undertone of coconut flavour.

Dried fruit: Dried fruit will give your granola a nice contrast of colour and texture while also adding some sweetness, but if you aren't a fan of dried fruit, simply leave it out. We use raisins and goji berries (for their vibrant red colour, but use them sparingly as they can sometimes be too hard or chewy) as well as chopped dried figs, dates, prunes, apricots and apple slices. Dried mango is another one of our favourites – use scissors to cut it into small pieces. As with the nuts and seeds, use whatever dried fruit you like or have on hand.

The key to using dried fruit in granola is to add it once the baked granola has come out of the oven and cooled completely, otherwise it will become even drier and tough, making it too hard and chewy.

The extras: If you want to take your granola to the next level, here are a few optional extras to add more variety and flavour:

- A pinch of ground cinnamon goes great with dried apples.

- Add some cacao powder for a chocolaty granola.

- Cacao nibs add a nice chocolaty flavour without the added fat and sugar.

- Coconut flakes, desiccated coconut and coconut milk powder add a subtle, milky, coconut undertone.

- Sometimes we also add a couple of tablespoons of ground flax seeds at the end, after the granola has come out of the oven and cooled, to add more body and nutrients.

- Freeze-dried raspberries or strawberries and chopped pistachios add pops of colour.

- Some extracts, such as almond extract, vanilla extract, orange oil, to add more concentrated flavour.

Texture: If you like granola that has big clusters in it, then it's as much about the process as it is the ingredients. So first of all, using a thicker, stickier sweetener, such as molasses, dark date syrup or really dark coconut blossom syrup, will help clusters to form. In addition, regular oat flakes cluster much better than jumbo oat flakes, so use small, regular oat flakes for better results.

Then, just before baking, when your granola is on the trays, use your hands or the back of a clean cup to pack down the granola and encourage it to form a flat, tight layer, which will help the oats, fat and sweetener to stick together. Once it's packed tightly and then baked, the granola will stick together into a 'blanket' that can be broken apart into clusters.

To make any of these granola recipes gluten free, simply use gluten-free oat flakes.

Makes approx. 1kg

1. Preheat the oven to 160°C fan/350°F/gas 4.

2. Chop the nuts (but not the flaked almonds) and coconut flakes (if using) if you like, or you can leave them whole.

3. Mix the oats, nuts, seeds and a tiny pinch of salt in a large bowl. Make sure you leave the dried fruit and any fancy extras aside, as they will be mixed in at the very end, once the granola is cool. If you prefer to eat your nuts raw, then leave them aside with your dried fruit, otherwise include them for a crunchier, more flavourful nut.

4. In a separate bowl or jug, mix the sweetener, oil and flavour agents (if using) together until well combined. Add to the dry mix in the bowl and mix thoroughly so that each oat flake, nut and seed gets an even coating.

5. Spread the granola out on a baking tray (or two if needed). Make sure the mix is spread out evenly if you want a nice crunchy granola – if it's not spread out evenly, it will steam as well as bake and result in some soft and some crunchy bits in your granola.

6. Bake in the preheated oven for 20 minutes, until golden brown, but you can bake it for longer if you prefer more of a crunch and a darker colour. The longer you leave it in the oven, the crunchier it will get up to the point where it will start to burn, so keep an eye on it to ensure you take it out before that happens!

7. Once the granola is baked, leave it to cool for at least 20 minutes. Make sure it really is cool before transferring to a large bowl and stirring in the dried fruit (and any optional extras from the list on p. 34).

8. Granola is great sprinkled on porridge or served on its own with non-dairy milk or yoghurt. Stored in an airtight container, it will easily keep for a few weeks.

RECIPE:	BASIC GRANOLA	FLUFFY COCONUT GRANOLA	CHOC NUT CRUNCH GRANOLA	MANGO, ORANGE AND GOJI GRANOLA
OATS	400g jumbo oat flakes	400g regular oat flakes	500g regular or jumbo oat flakes	500g regular oat flakes
NUTS	70g cashews 30g flaked almonds	50g flaked almonds 30g pecans 20g coconut flakes	50g Brazil nuts 50g hazelnuts	50g walnuts 30g cashews 20g flaked almonds
SEEDS	100g pumpkin seeds	50g pumpkin seeds 50g sunflower seeds	40g pumpkin seeds 40g sesame seeds 20g chia seeds	40g pumpkin seeds 30g sesame seeds 30g sunflower seeds
SALT	Pinch of salt	Pinch of salt	Pinch of salt	Pinch of salt
SWEETENER	150ml date syrup	100ml maple syrup	150ml brown rice syrup	150ml maple syrup
OIL	80ml sunflower oil	80g coconut oil, melted	80ml sunflower oil	80ml sunflower oil
FLAVOUR AGENTS		1 tsp vanilla extract	25g cocoa powder 1 tsp almond extract	1 tsp orange essence
DRIED FRUIT	50g raisins 30g goji berries 20g sultanas	100g raisins 10g freeze-dried raspberries	40g dried figs, chopped 30g dried apples 30g sultanas	50g dried mango, chopped 30g dried apricots, chopped 20g goji berries

BREAKDOWN ↑↓

HOMEMADE NON-DAIRY MILK

Making your own non-dairy milk couldn't be easier, plus the beauty of making your own is that it's raw, unfiltered and unsweetened (unless, of course, you want to add some sweetener). It also eliminates packaging.

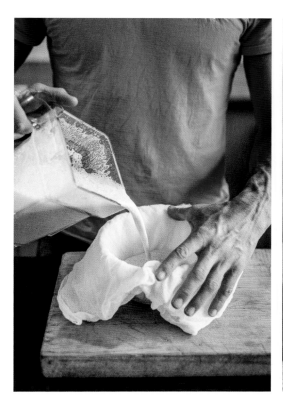

Makes 1 litre

1. If you're making the almond or oat milk, soak the flavour agent (the almonds or oats) overnight in the 800ml of water along with the dates if you're using the optional sweetener.

2. If you're making the almond milk (or if you're using any type of nut for a nut milk), it's important to drain and rinse the nuts, as all nuts will release an enzyme inhibitor and some acid into the soaking water. By rinsing them you are rinsing away this bitter flavour. (You don't have to do this with oats, rice, quinoa or any other grain.) Put the drained and rinsed nuts and the soaked dates (if using) into a high-speed blender with 800ml of fresh water and blend until reasonably smooth.

3. If you're making the oat, rice or quinoa milk, include the soaked oat, rice or quinoa along with the soak water, emulsifier (if using), a small pinch of salt and the sweetener (if using) and blend until reasonably smooth.

4. Put a cheesecloth, muslin or even a clean J-cloth into a sieve set over a large bowl or pot and pour in the blended liquid, pressing on and squeezing the pulp to get out every last drop of milk.

5. Transfer to a clean 1 litre bottle, seal with a lid and store in the fridge for up to 3 days.

RECIPE:	ALMOND MILK	OAT MILK	RICE MILK	QUINOA MILK
FLAVOUR AGENT	200g almonds	200g rolled oats	200g cooked white or brown rice (p. 301; white rice is naturally sweeter)	200g cooked quinoa (p. 301)
WATER	800ml water	800ml water	800ml water	800ml water
EMULSIFIER		1 tsp sunflower oil	1 tsp sunflower oil	
SALT		Small pinch of salt	Small pinch of salt	Small pinch of salt
SWEETENER (OPTIONAL)	4 pitted dates	2 pitted dates		2 pitted dates

BREAKDOWN ↑ ↓

PANCAKES

Pancakes are a crowd-pleaser going back 30,000 years, when they were most likely cooked on a heated rock! The recipe hasn't changed too much since then. From the Ancient Greek or Roman version to the modern-day French crêpe, delightfully fluffy American blueberry pancakes and the annual Pancake Tuesday version with lemon and sugar, pancakes are simple and satisfying.

In essence, a pancake is a flat cake cooked in a pan. It can be made into an indulgent sweet treat or a healthier version, but first you need to understand the basics and the framework, so we've broken down the traditional flour, milk and egg batter to help empower you to make a variety of delicious vegan versions with confidence and ease. The essential approach that we apply to pancakes is based around 120g (1 cup) of flour, which should make 4 to 6 pancakes (that's our Basic recipe in the framework).

THE ESSENTIALS

Flour: In general, use an equal portion of flour to liquid in terms of volume (i.e. 1 cup flour to 1 cup liquid), but in weight it is one part flour to two parts liquid. This will work with most flours, with the exception of coconut flour and gluten-free white flours. Also, wholemeal flour will typically need 10% more liquid compared to white flour, as it's higher in fibre.

We call for plain white flour in the recipes here, but personally we prefer to use a wholemeal flour as it is much higher in fibre and more nutritious overall than a plain white flour. Wholemeal flour is denser than white flour, so it might require more raising agent. As a general rule of thumb, we use at least 1 teaspoon of baking powder per 120g of wholemeal flour.

Liquid:

- **Non-dairy milk:** Use a non-dairy milk of choice, such as oat, rice or almond milk.

- **Apple juice:** Apple juice adds a little extra flavour and will also result in a much sweeter pancake. It works better in crêpes, as it's thinner than the other liquids listed here.

- **Tinned coconut milk:** Coconut milk is a good way to add a subtle coconut flavour as well as fat to your pancakes for extra richness and indulgence.

Binder: In a traditional pancake, the binder that holds the starch (flour) and liquid together is the egg, but there are plenty of other options to choose from in vegan cooking. The main binders we use in pancakes are:

- **Almond butter or light tahini:** We use 3 tablespoons for this framework.

- **Ground flax seeds or ground chia seeds:** 2 tablespoons is the norm for this framework.

- **Mashed banana:** One mashed banana works well in this framework.

- **Cooked pumpkin, squash or sweet potato:** Use 50g of any of these.

Sweetener: We usually add 2 tablespoons of sweetener to the basic pancake recipe.

Fat: A little oil is completely optional, but it will make your pancakes more rich and indulgent. If you're aiming for a light, fluffy pancake, use coconut oil. Limit the fat to 1 tablespoon for our base recipe of 120g of flour.

Raising agent: Baking powder helps baked goods to rise and is what makes your pancake develop little bubbles as it's cooking. If you omit it, no bubbles or air pockets form, which means your pancakes are much more likely to burn. We typically add 1 teaspoon of baking powder per 120g of flour.

Flavour agents: Play around with flavourings, such as vanilla or almond extract, ground coffee, coconut, spices, berries, chocolate chips, orange zest or a little juice to replace some of the liquid.

Salt: A small pinch of salt helps to balance the sweetener.

CLASSIC PANCAKES

Makes 4 to 6 medium pancakes or crêpes

Using one recipe and simply adjusting the amount of liquid, you can create three different pancakes: a basic pancake, a light and fluffy American-style pancake and a thin French-style crêpe.

Any of these batters will also work for waffles – all you need is a waffle iron, which you can buy online or in most electrical stores. Or if you have a sandwich or grill iron, they often come with waffle plates too. (See a picture of some tasty-looking waffles on p. 46!)

1. Put all the ingredients except the oil into a blender and blend until smooth, or whisk together in a large bowl. Leave to sit for a couple of minutes.

2. Heat the oil in a large non-stick frying pan on a medium heat until it's warm. If making the basic or American-style pancakes, pour 5 to 8 tablespoons of batter into the pan per pancake and don't spread them out. When bubbles or air pockets start to appear and the top of the pancake starts to dry out, it's time to turn them (a small silicone spatula will help to flip them). Turn your pancakes over and cook for 1 minute more, until golden.

3. If you're making crêpes, pour a small ladleful of batter into the middle of the pan, then tilt the pan until the batter covers the base in a thin layer. Cook for 60 to 90 seconds, until set and golden, then use a silicone spatula to flip it over. Cook the other side for about 60 seconds, until golden.

4. Pancakes are very plain on their own, so get creative with toppings. Typical toppings include a dollop of non-dairy yoghurt, fruit compote or stewed fruit (see p. 26), fresh fruit or berries or caramelized banana (see p. 49), and don't forget a generous drizzle of maple syrup or your favourite sweetener. If making crêpes, try chocolate hazelnut spread and sliced bananas for a real treat. When we were kids our mom sprinkled caster sugar and lemon on our pancakes, so every time we eat them that way now, we feel like six-year-old boys again!

RECIPE:	BASIC PANCAKES	LIGHT AND FLUFFY AMERICAN-STYLE PANCAKES	FRENCH-STYLE CRÊPES
FLOUR	120g plain white flour	120g plain white flour	120g plain white flour
LIQUID	260ml oat milk	200ml oat milk	300ml oat milk
BINDER	2 tbsp ground flax seeds	2 tbsp ground flax seeds	2 tbsp ground flax seeds
SWEETENER	2 tbsp maple syrup	2 tbsp maple syrup	2 tbsp maple syrup
RAISING AGENT	1 tsp baking powder	1½ tsp baking powder	1 tsp baking powder
FLAVOUR AGENT	1 tsp vanilla extract	1 tsp vanilla extract	1 tsp vanilla extract
SALT	Pinch of salt	Pinch of salt	Pinch of salt
OIL	½ tsp oil	½ tsp oil	½ tsp oil

BREAKDOWN ↑ ↓

PANCAKE VARIATIONS

Makes 4 to 6 medium pancakes

Once you have the basics down, this framework takes it to the next level with four different flavours and styles of pancakes. You can find chickpea/gram flour in health food shops or some supermarkets and you can get pumpkin purée in some larger supermarkets.

Follow the instructions for making and cooking the basic pancakes on p. 44, but with the following changes to make the batter:

1. American-style blueberry pancakes: If whisking all the ingredients by hand instead of blending, whisk the milk and mashed banana together before adding all the other ingredients. Don't blend the blueberries with the rest of the ingredients, but rather stir them into the batter at the end.

2. Pumpkin and buckwheat pancakes: If whisking all the ingredients by hand instead of blending, whisk the milk and pumpkin together before adding all the other ingredients.

3. Chocolate and orange spelt pancakes: If whisking all the ingredients by hand instead of blending, whisk the milk and tahini together before adding all the other ingredients. Don't blend the chocolate chips and orange zest, but rather add a little to each pancake once you have cooked one side and are cooking the other side so that the chocolate has enough time to melt but not burn.

4. Serve the blueberry, buckwheat and spelt pancakes as per the suggestions on p. 44. We like to serve the savoury chickpea pancakes with hummus and salads.

$\rightarrow$

RECIPE:	AMERICAN-STYLE BLUEBERRY PANCAKES	PUMPKIN AND BUCKWHEAT PANCAKES	CHOCOLATE AND ORANGE SPELT PANCAKES	SAVOURY SPICED CHICKPEA PANCAKES
FLOUR	120g plain white flour	120g buckwheat flour	120g wholemeal spelt flour	120g chickpea/gram flour
LIQUID	135ml rice milk	300ml rice milk	210ml oat milk	210ml oat milk
BINDER	1 ripe banana, mashed	3 tbsp pumpkin purée	3 tbsp tahini	
SWEETENER	2 tbsp maple syrup	2 tbsp maple syrup	2 tbsp maple syrup	
FAT				1 tbsp oil
RAISING AGENT	2 tsp baking powder	1 tsp baking powder	1 tsp baking powder	1 tsp baking powder
FLAVOUR AGENTS	75g blueberries ½ tsp vanilla extract	¼ tsp ground cinnamon ¼ tsp ground nutmeg ¼ tsp vanilla extract	40g dark chocolate chips Zest of 1 orange	½ tsp ground cumin ½ tsp ground coriander ½ tsp garlic powder
SALT	Pinch of salt	Pinch of salt	Pinch of salt	Pinch of salt
OIL	½ tsp oil	½ tsp oil	½ tsp oil	½ tsp oil

BREAKDOWN ↑ ↓

CARAMELIZED BANANA

Caramelizing a banana is such a simple thing to do and takes only a few minutes, but it can really transform a breakfast. We love to serve caramelized banana with porridge for a sense of decadence, and it always looks so impressive too.

The most important thing here is to ensure that your bananas are really ripe, even overripe – they should be starting to develop brown spots. For anything to caramelize you need sugar, and the riper the banana is, the more sugar is available to caramelize.

So to caramelize a banana . . .

1. Put a non-stick frying pan on a high heat. Once the pan is hot, reduce the heat to medium.

2. Peel the banana and slice it in half lengthways, then put it into the pan face down.

3. Cook for 1 or 2 minutes, until it starts to brown and caramelize.

4. Turn it over (a silicone spatula works best for this) and repeat on the other side.

5. Sprinkle over a pinch of ground cinnamon if you like, and serve on top of porridge, pancakes or whatever takes your fancy.

OMELETTE AND FRITTATA

How do you replace the eggs to make a vegan omelette or frittata? The answer may sound a little strange, but it's a mixture of tofu, chickpea flour (also known as gram flour) and a little ground turmeric for colour, but the results look and taste remarkably close to the real thing.

An omelette and a frittata both have fillings and are 'egg' based, but an omelette is usually made to serve just one, is thinner than a frittata and is folded over in half, with the filling inside. A frittata will feed a number of people and is a heartier cousin of the omelette, more like a crustless quiche that's loaded up with fillings – the Spanish tortilla de patatas is the perfect example. A frittata is usually started on the hob, then finished off in the same pan in the oven. Delicious served hot or cold.

THE ESSENTIALS

Silken tofu: Protein-rich and creamy, silken tofu is softer than firm tofu.

Black sulphur salt: Also known as kala namak or Himalayan black salt, this salt adds an eggy flavour due to its sulphur content. It really makes your omelette or frittata taste like its non-vegan counterpart.

Nutritional yeast: For a cheesy dairy flavour.

Chickpea/gram flour: This bulks up the texture. Chickpea/gram flour has a natural yellow colour, plus due to its higher protein content it easily forms an egg-like texture.

Fillings

Use your own favourite fillings. Some of our favourites are cherry tomatoes, sautéed greens, wilted spinach, fresh rocket, pan-fried mushrooms, roasted peppers, diced leftover potatoes, pesto, and vegan feta if you can source it.

OMELETTE

Makes 1 omelette

1. First, prepare your filling so that it's ready to add when you need it, as omelettes cook quickly. Raw fillings such as rocket, baby spinach, halved cherry tomatoes and pesto can be added directly to the cooked omelette. For cooked fillings, peel and slice the veg, such as onions, garlic, mushrooms, peppers, kale or cooked leftover potatoes.

2. Heat 1 tablespoon of olive oil in a frying pan on a medium heat. Add your veg and cook for 10 minutes, stirring occasionally, until cooked through. Set aside.

3. Drain the tofu to remove any liquid, then put all the ingredients except for the filling, oil and seasoning into a food processor or blender and blend until smooth, or whisk together by hand in a large bowl.

4. Heat the oil in a non-stick frying pan (or an ovenproof non-stick pan if you're going to finish your omelette in the oven) on a low to medium heat to give your omelette a lovely golden base without cooking too quickly. When the oil is hot, pour the omelette mixture into the pan, tilting the pan to get it to spread over the entire base. Cook for 5 minutes without stirring, then, using a small silicone spatula, gently lift up an edge to see if the bottom of your omelette is golden brown.

5. Spread the filling over one half of the omelette, then gently fold over the other half to seal it in. Reduce the heat to low and cook for 2 to 3 minutes more, until firm and cooked through. (Or, if your omelette-flipping skills are a little lacking, you don't need to fold your omelette – simply add your filling in an even layer over the entire surface, then transfer the pan to the oven preheated to 160°C fan/350°F/gas 4 and cook for 10 minutes, until firm and cooked through.)

6. Season with a little black sulphur salt to taste (if you don't have sulphur salt just use normal salt). The sulphur salt will add an eggy taste that tends to diminish when cooked, so it's best to add it just before serving to maintain the flavour.

7. Slide the omelette out of the pan on to a plate and serve straight away.

RECIPE:	BASIC OMELETTE	OMELETTE WITH MUSHROOMS AND WILTED SPINACH	OMELETTE WITH BASIL PESTO AND CHERRY TOMATOES
FILLING		100g mushrooms 1 onion Handful of baby spinach 1 garlic clove 1 tbsp oil	3 tbsp basil pesto (p. 167) 5 cherry tomatoes, halved or quartered
TOFU	175g silken tofu	175g silken tofu	175g silken tofu
STARCH	20g chickpea/gram flour 1 tbsp arrowroot/cornflour	20g chickpea/gram flour 1 tbsp arrowroot/cornflour	20g chickpea/gram flour 1 tbsp arrowroot/cornflour
LIQUID	4 tbsp oat milk	4 tbsp oat milk	4 tbsp oat milk
FLAVOUR AGENTS	2 tbsp nutritional yeast ¼ tsp ground turmeric (for colour)	2 tbsp nutritional yeast ¼ tsp ground turmeric (for colour)	2 tbsp nutritional yeast ¼ tsp ground turmeric (for colour)
TEXTURE ENHANCER	1 tbsp light tahini	1 tbsp light tahini	1 tbsp light tahini
OIL	1 tsp olive oil	1 tsp olive oil	1 tsp olive oil
SEASONING (TO TASTE)	Pinch of black sulphur salt or fine sea salt	Pinch of black sulphur salt or fine sea salt	Pinch of black sulphur salt or fine sea salt

← BREAKDOWN →

FRITTATA

Serves 4 to 6

Our frittata has similar ingredients to the omelette on p. 52, but with the extra addition of aquafaba (the water from tinned chickpeas) to lighten it up and bind it together. While it won't look exactly like the usual egg mixture going into the pan, it will give you a frittata that looks and tastes like the real thing.

1. Preheat the oven to 180°C fan/400°F/gas 6.

2. If you're making the roast veg frittata, cut the veg into bite-size pieces. Place on a baking tray, drizzle with the tablespoon of oil, season with a pinch of salt and roast in the preheated oven for 25 minutes.

3. If you're making the potato frittata, leave the skin on the potatoes and cut them in half so that they are all a similar size. Bring a large saucepan or pot of salted water to the boil and put a steamer over it. Put the potatoes into the steamer, cover with a lid and steam for 20 minutes. Check to see if they're cooked by inserting the tip of a small sharp knife into the middle of the biggest potato – if it glides through easily, they're cooked. If it's still a little hard, steam for another few minutes. You want the potatoes to be cooked through but not falling apart. Remove from the heat and when they're cool enough to handle, cut into slices 5mm thick.

4. While your potatoes are steaming, peel your onions, cut them in half, then slice them into thin half-moons. Heat the oil in a large non-stick ovenproof frying pan on a low to medium heat, then add the onions and cook for 15 minutes, stirring occasionally. Remove from the pan and set aside.

5. Drain the tofu to remove any liquid, then put all the ingredients except for the filling, oil and seasoning into a food processor or blender and blend until smooth, or whisk together by hand in a large bowl.

6. Heat the oil in a small (18cm) non-stick ovenproof frying pan on a low to medium heat. When the oil is hot, pour half the frittata mixture into the pan, tilting the pan to get it to spread over the entire base. Cook for 2 minutes, then add half the filling evenly over the top. Add the remaining frittata mixture and cook for 2 minutes more, then add the remaining filling on top. Continue to cook for 5 minutes, until it looks like it's starting to set, then transfer the pan to the oven for 30 minutes to finish cooking.

7. Season with a little black sulphur salt to taste (if you don't have sulphur salt, just use normal salt). The sulphur salt will add an eggy taste that tends to diminish when cooked, so it's best to add it just before serving to maintain the flavour.

8. Now it's time to invert the frittata, so cover your pan with a large plate and carefully flip it upside down, out of the pan and on to the plate. Allow to sit for 5 to 10 minutes before slicing. Serve warm or cold, with your favourite salad.

RECIPE:	ROAST VEG FRITTATA	POTATO FRITTATA
FILLING	400g peppers 250g leeks ½ a small courgette 1 tbsp oil Pinch of salt	500g potatoes 200g onions 1 tbsp oil
TOFU	220g silken tofu	220g silken tofu
STARCH	60g chickpea/gram flour 2 tsp arrowroot/cornflour	25g chickpea/gram flour 2 tsp arrowroot/cornflour
LIQUID	2 tbsp oat milk	3½ tbsp oat milk
FLAVOUR AGENTS	4 tbsp nutritional yeast ¼ tsp smoked paprika ¼ tsp ground turmeric (for colour)	4 tbsp nutritional yeast ¼ tsp smoked paprika ¼ tsp ground turmeric (for colour)
TEXTURE ENHANCER	25ml aquafaba	75ml aquafaba
OIL	1 tbsp olive oil	1 tbsp olive oil
SEASONING (TO TASTE)	½ tsp black sulphur salt or fine sea salt	½ tsp black sulphur salt or fine sea salt

BREAKDOWN ←→

SCRAMBLED EGGS

Serves 1 to 2

If you want to re-create the actual flavour of egg, a vital ingredient is black sulphur salt, also known as kala namak or Himalayan black salt. It really adds an eggy flavour and will genuinely surprise and delight you when it comes to making vegan eggs. You can buy it online and we really recommend sourcing it if you want to make vegan omelettes, frittatas or scrambled eggs.

1. Drain the tofu to remove any liquid, then put it into a bowl and mash until crumbled (but don't crumble it too much or overmix if using the silken tofu).

2. Sift the starch (if using) into the tofu and briefly stir to combine.

3. Mix the flavour agents together in a small bowl, then add to the crumbled tofu, stirring just until the tofu is evenly coated.

4. Heat the oil in a non-stick frying pan on a medium heat. Once the oil is hot, turn the heat down to low and add the tofu mixture to the pan. Move the mixture around the pan with a spatula, allowing it to cook gently and slowly for 3 to 4 minutes, until it has slightly browned and firmed up.

5. Season with the black sulphur salt (if you don't have sulphur salt, just use normal salt). The sulphur salt will add an eggy taste that tends to diminish when cooked, so it's best to add it just before serving to maintain the flavour.

6. Serve the scrambled eggs immediately on your favourite toast, or as part of a vegan fry.

BREAKDOWN ↑↓	**RECIPE:**	**BASIC SCRAMBLED EGGS**	**SILKY SCRAMBLED EGGS**
	TOFU	200g firm tofu	100g silken tofu 100g firm tofu
	STARCH		2 tbsp chickpea/gram flour
	FLAVOUR AGENTS	1 tbsp tamari or soy sauce ¼ tsp onion powder ¼ tsp ground turmeric (for colour)	1 tbsp tamari or soy sauce ¼ tsp onion powder ¼ tsp ground turmeric (for colour)
	OIL	1 tbsp olive oil	1 tbsp olive oil
	SEASONING (TO TASTE)	⅓ tsp black sulphur salt	⅓ tsp black sulphur salt

BACON

Serves 2 to 4

While we can't re-create bacon, we can replicate that irresistible smoky, salty/sweet flavour and moreish umami using different veg or proteins as the flavour carriers. The coconut bacon is more like a lovely crispy snack than a proper bacon substitute – it goes great in salads or as a garnish, or even in sandwiches.

1. Slice the base ingredient (tempeh, mushrooms or aubergine) into long, very thin strips (aim for 5mm thick at the most), so that all the strips/pieces are around the same size (there's no need to slice the coconut).

2. Whisk together all the remaining ingredients except the oil in a bowl to make the marinade. Spread the marinade evenly on both sides of the base ingredient. The longer you leave it to marinate, the stronger the flavour will be. If you have time let it marinate in the fridge overnight, but if not, even 10 minutes is good.

3. Heat the oil in a non-stick frying pan on a medium heat. Add the bacon strips and cook for a few minutes on each side, until nicely browned. If you're making the aubergine bacon, make sure it's fully cooked through and reaches a melt-in-your-mouth texture. With the tempeh and mushrooms you want to cook each side so that they start to brown and char. If you're making the coconut bacon, cook until it's almost crisp in texture. Serve hot.

RECIPE:	TEMPEH BACON	MUSHROOM BACON	AUBERGINE BACON	COCONUT BACON
BASE	150g tempeh	150g mushrooms	150g aubergine	160g coconut flakes
UMAMI	4 tbsp tamari or soy sauce	4 tbsp tamari or soy sauce	4 tbsp tamari or soy sauce	4 tbsp tamari or soy sauce
ACID	2 tbsp apple cider vinegar	2 tbsp apple cider vinegar	2 tbsp apple cider vinegar	2 tbsp apple cider vinegar
WATER	2 tbsp water	2 tbsp water	2 tbsp water	
SWEETENER	2 tsp maple syrup	2 tsp maple syrup	2 tsp maple syrup	2 tsp maple syrup
SMOKY	2 tsp smoked paprika	2 tsp smoked paprika	2 tsp smoked paprika	2 tsp smoked paprika
FLAVOUR AGENTS	3 tbsp tomato purée 1 tsp garlic powder	3 tbsp tomato purée 1 tsp garlic powder	3 tbsp tomato purée 1 tsp garlic powder	1 tsp garlic powder
SALT	Pinch of salt	Pinch of salt	Pinch of salt	Pinch of salt
OIL	1 tbsp olive oil	1 tbsp olive oil	1 tbsp olive oil	1 tbsp olive oil

BREAKDOWN

SAUSAGES

Makes 8 to 10

These look fab and taste great in a vegan fry or with creamy mash and gravy (see p. 261). This framework shows you how to make two different but tasty versions of a vegan sausage.

1. If you're making the sweet potato and quinoa sausages, drain and rinse the beans. Peel and finely chop the onion and garlic. Chop the cashews finely into very small pieces.

2. If you're making the cheesy sun-dried tomato, basil and parsnip sausages, soak the sun-dried tomatoes in just-boiled water for 5 minutes, then drain and finely dice. Strip the basil leaves from the stalks, then discard the stalks and finely chop the leaves. Grate the vegan Cheddar. Chop the cashews finely into very small pieces.

3. Put the grain/beans, cooked veg, flavour agents, fat, spices and seasoning into a large bowl. Mash together until everything is nicely broken down and well incorporated. Alternatively, use a food processor and blend until chunky if you want a bit of a bite, or blend until completely smooth.

4. Stir in the binder ingredients – the mixture should hold its shape.

5. Portion into 50g to 75g balls, then roll each ball into a 12.5cm-long sausage shape. Roll in sesame seeds if you want the sausages to have a crust.

6. Heat the oil in a large non-stick frying pan on a medium heat. Working in batches to ensure that the sausages all have enough room to touch the bottom of the pan, cook until nicely browned on all sides and completely heated through. Alternatively, you could coat the sausages in a small amount of oil and roast them on a tray or in a baking dish in an oven preheated to 170°C fan/375°F/gas 5 for 15 to 20 minutes.

7. Serve hot as part of a complete vegan fry with all the trimmings.

BREAKDOWN	RECIPE:	SWEET POTATO AND QUINOA SAUSAGES	CHEESY SUN-DRIED TOMATO, BASIL AND PARSNIP SAUSAGES
	GRAIN / BEANS	150g cooked quinoa or couscous (p. 301) 120g tinned borlotti or mixed beans	120g cooked quinoa (p. 301)
	COOKED VEG	100g roasted sweet potato (p. 300)	300g cooked parsnips or celeriac (pp. 298 & 300)
	FLAVOUR AGENTS	1 red onion 1 garlic clove 1 tbsp tamari or soy sauce	50g sun-dried tomatoes (the dried kind, not the ones in oil) 25g fresh basil
	FAT	50g cashews	75g vegan Cheddar cheese 65g cashews
	SPICES	½ tsp dried rosemary ½ tsp dried mixed herbs ¼ tsp chilli powder	½ tsp onion powder ¼ tsp chilli powder
	SEASONING (TO TASTE)	1 tsp salt ½ tsp freshly ground black pepper	1 tsp salt ½ tsp freshly ground black pepper
	BINDER	4 tsp rice flour 4 tsp psyllium husks	4 tsp rice flour 4 tsp psyllium husks
	SESAME SEEDS (OPTIONAL)	25g sesame seeds	25g sesame seeds
	OIL	1 tbsp olive oil	1 tbsp olive oil

EPIC BAKED BEANS

Serves 4

The good news is that baked beans are usually vegan – and are always delicious! Beans on toast is an old favourite and is such a satisfying and substantial protein hit, and once you make your own you'll never go back to tins. These homemade baked beans are also delicious as part of a vegan fry. After you try the basic recipe, experiment with the other two variations.

1. To prepare the base veg, peel and finely chop the onions and garlic. Deseed and finely chop the chillies (if using). Drain and rinse the beans.

2. Heat the oil in a medium saucepan on a medium heat. Add the base veg and cook for 3 to 5 minutes, stirring occasionally, until translucent. Add the beans, stirring to allow them to absorb the flavours of the onion, garlic and chilli (if using).

3. Add all the sauce ingredients along with the sweetener, acid and seasoning. Mix well so that all the flavours are mixed together and incorporated. Reduce the heat to low and simmer for 5 to 10 minutes, until the sauce has reduced slightly and the flavours have blended together.

4. Your delicious homemade beans are now ready to serve on toast or as part of a vegan fry.

RECIPE:	BASIC BAKED BEANS	BBQ BAKED BEANS	SPICY BAKED BEANS
BASE VEG	2 medium onions 2 garlic cloves 1 to 2 tbsp oil	2 medium onions 2 garlic cloves 1 to 2 tbsp oil	2 medium onions 2 garlic cloves 2 fresh red chillies 1 to 2 tbsp oil
BEANS	2 × 400g tins of cannellini or mixed beans	2 × 400g tins of cannellini or mixed beans	2 × 400g tins of cannellini or mixed beans
SAUCE	1 × 680g jar of passata or tomato sauce ½ tsp chilli powder	1 × 680g jar of passata or tomato sauce 2 tbsp tamari or soy sauce 2 tbsp ketchup (p. 322) 2 tbsp maple syrup 1 tsp smoked paprika 1 tsp Dijon mustard ½ tsp chilli powder	1 × 680g jar of passata or tomato sauce 2 tbsp tamari or soy sauce 2 tbsp ketchup (p. 322) 2 tbsp maple syrup 2 tsp chilli powder 1 tsp cayenne pepper 1 tsp Dijon mustard
SWEETENER	3 tbsp maple syrup	3 tbsp maple syrup	3 tbsp maple syrup
ACID	3 tbsp apple cider vinegar	3 tbsp apple cider vinegar	3 tbsp apple cider vinegar
SEASONING	3 tbsp tamari or soy sauce 2 tsp salt	3 tbsp tamari or soy sauce 2 tsp salt	3 tbsp tamari or soy sauce 2 tsp salt

BREAKDOWN

GREENS

Serves 1 to 2

Cooked greens are a healthy and tasty addition to a vegan fry and they help to balance the dish. You can interchange the greens depending on what's in season.

RECIPE:	SPINACH	SWISS CHARD OR KALE	PAK CHOI
OIL	1 tbsp olive oil	1 tbsp olive oil	1 tbsp olive oil
GREENS	200g spinach	200g Swiss chard or kale	1 head of pak choi (or 2 heads if using only the greens)
FLAVOUR AGENTS AND SEASONING	Juice of ½ a lemon 1 tsp salt ½ tsp freshly grated nutmeg	1 or 2 garlic cloves 1 tbsp tamari or soy sauce	1 or 2 garlic cloves 1 medium fresh chilli 1 tbsp tamari or soy sauce

(left margin label: ↑ BREAKDOWN ↓)

1. To prepare Swiss chard or kale, strip the leaves off the hard stalks, then discard the stalks and roughly chop the leaves. Roughly chop the pak choi. Peel and finely chop the garlic (if using). Deseed the chilli (if using) if you don't want as much heat, and finely chop.

2. Heat the oil in a medium to large frying pan on a medium heat. Add the garlic and chilli (if using) and cook for 2 to 3 minutes, stirring. Add your greens and cook for 2 or 3 minutes more, until wilted or softened. Add the flavour agents and seasoning and cook for 1 minute more (if making the spinach, add the lemon juice at the very end of the cooking time).

3. Taste and adjust the seasoning – they might need more salt or acid. Serve immediately.

Soup

We hope to inspire you to love soup as much as we do! We find soup to be simple yet elegant, and there can be something so nourishing and wholesome about it – a good soup can feel like it's feeding your soul.

We've made soups in our cafés for more than a decade and have never used a recipe. Instead, we use a framework. This means that we can always use any new produce that comes in or try out any crazy ideas we have. If there are lots of ripe pumpkins that need to be used up, or if someone drops in a load of wild garlic, we can always adapt and make a fab soup. Once you learn our core soup frameworks for smooth and chunky soups, you won't need a recipe again either. Soup empowerment is within your grasp!

THE ESSENTIALS

Base veg: More often than not, we use a standard base veg for our soups. This usually constitutes about 20% of the total volume of the soup. In other words, if you're making 4 litres of soup (which would make 8 × 500ml servings), your base veg would be 750g in total. The base veg of our soups usually consists of equal portions (approx. 250g each) of onions, carrots and celeriac. We use celeriac rather than the more traditional celery used in a classic French mirepoix, as we find that celeriac gives more body to soups than celery but still has a similar flavour. A mirepoix is a mix made up of 50% onion, 25% carrot and 25% celery, all diced up finely and cooked on a low heat until it becomes sweet rather than fried for caramelization. However, we like to use equal proportions of onions, carrots and celeriac and we normally roast them in the cafés, but sweating works great too.

Liquid: The liquid element will usually constitute 50% to 60% of the total volume of the soup (note that when it comes to water and many other liquids, the amounts in grams and millilitres are the same, i.e. 1 litre of water = 1kg). The liquid is usually veg stock or water, but you could add some coconut milk or tinned tomatoes instead for additional flavour or colour, which will also make up some of the liquid volume of the soup. But if you're using good-quality fresh veg, you can easily get away without using veg stock and just use water as your liquid. For our standard batch of 4 litres of soup, you will use 2 to 2.5 litres of liquid/veg stock.

We make our own veg stock in our cafés but we tend not to make it at home; instead, we use a good-quality, low-sodium veg bouillon powder. However, if you want to have a go at making your own, see our notes on making homemade veg stock on p. 303.

Hero ingredients: The hero ingredients will be the predominant flavour of your soup (and will also affect the final colour). The hero ingredients usually make up 20% of the volume of the soup (but can obviously be more – just reduce the base veg if adding more hero ingredients), so a little less than one-quarter of your pot will be made up of your hero ingredients. Here are a few examples of some winner smooth soup combinations to give you a better idea of what we mean by hero ingredients:

- Broccoli, sweet potato and ginger

- Carrot, cashew and coriander

- Roasted root veg and thyme

- Squash, coconut and ginger

- Sweet potato, coconut and lemongrass

Flavour agents: These are the things that will add an additional element and give a greater depth of flavour to your soup.

- Tamari: Add with the hero ingredients.

- Fresh herbs: Add picked fresh thyme, chopped basil, coriander, parsley, etc. at the end, just before serving.

- Miso: Add at the end, just before serving.

- Citrus: Add a squeeze of lemon or lime juice or some zest at the end, just before serving.

- Fresh ginger: Add a thumb-size piece of fresh ginger, peeled and finely chopped, with the base veg or hero ingredients. (If using organic ginger, we never peel it, as lots of the goodness is in the skin.)

- Chilli: Deseed a fresh chilli (or keep the seeds if you don't mind the extra heat) and finely chop, then add with the base veg or hero ingredients.

- Coconut milk: This is both a flavour agent and a liquid. Add it with the other liquid for extra creaminess and sweetness.

- Chopped tomatoes: These are both a flavour agent and a liquid. Add them with the other liquid.

- Nuts: Add with the hero ingredients for extra creaminess, as nuts are typically 50% fat.

- Nut or seed butters: Add with the hero ingredients for extra creaminess and richness.

- Seaweed: Add some kelp or dulse/dillisk with the base veg for some natural saltiness and to increase the mineral content.

- Some spices we like to use in soups:
  - Ground cumin and ground coriander give a nice warming element to your soup.
  - Paprika adds a nice red colour to your soup but doesn't really affect the taste.
  - Smoked paprika works well in chunky lentil soups and adds a smoky, beefy flavour, but it's strong so use it sparingly.
  - Curry powder lends some spice and usually changes the colour to yellow.
  - Turmeric changes the colour to yellow and also adds an astringent, slightly bitter note, so use it sparingly.
  - Cinnamon and cardamom add an aromatic and fragrant note to the soup.

Seasoning: Season the soup to your own taste using salt, pepper and spices. Start by adding just a little, then taste and keep adjusting until it suits your preference.

Garnish

A nice garnish can really elevate a soup. Here are some garnishes that we like to use:

- Flaked almonds

- Chopped nuts (any type)

- A drizzle of non-dairy yoghurt (works great against bright, vibrant soups, such as a beetroot or carrot soup)

- A drizzle of a flavoured oil, such as chilli oil or lemon oil

- Fresh herbs, such as thyme leaves, chopped chives, coriander leaves, basil leaves, parsley leaves, etc.

- Chilli flakes add a nice pop of colour and add a kick of heat too

- Toasted seeds

- Gomashio (a Japanese condiment of sesame seeds and salt – see p. 310 for the recipe)

- Vegetable crisps, such as sweet potato or parsnip crisps, or a thinly sliced roasted vegetable

- Pink peppercorns add a vibrant pop of colour and work particularly well with green-coloured soups, but use them sparingly as they will affect the taste

SMOOTH SOUP

We base our smooth soup framework around a 4-litre pot of soup, which will give you 8 × 500ml servings. To make a smooth soup you will need an immersion blender or some other means of blending your soup. The following is our framework for a smooth soup:

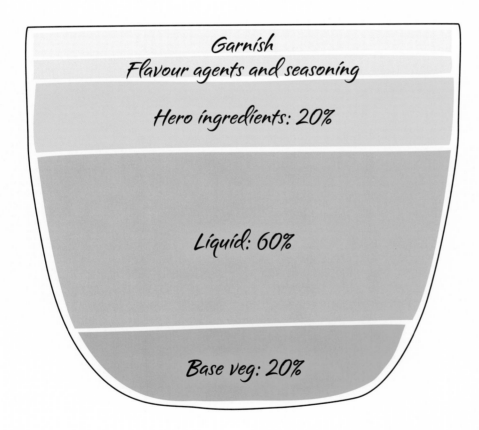

Garnish
Flavour agents and seasoning

Hero ingredients: 20%

Liquid: 60%

Base veg: 20%

Makes 4 litres (8 x 500ml servings)

1. Peel and roughly chop your base veg and any veg in the hero ingredients into even-sized pieces. (To keep its colour pale we omit carrots from the base veg in our mushroom soup, p. 83.)

2. Heat the oil in a large saucepan on a high heat. Add the base veg to the pan and cook, stirring, for a couple of minutes. Reduce to a medium heat, add a good pinch of salt, then put a lid on the pan and cook for a further 10 minutes, stirring occasionally. The veg will essentially steam in their own juices, making them soft, tender and succulent.

3. Alternatively, to bake your base veg, preheat the oven to 180°C fan/400°F/ gas 6. Spread the chopped veg out on a baking tray, then drizzle with the oil, sprinkle over a pinch of salt and toss to coat. Bake in the preheated oven for 25 minutes, until tender. Baking tends to make your veg sweeter, as it reduces the moisture through the baking process. It can also brown or caramelize the edges of the veg, giving a nice extra flavour dimension. If we bake the base veg, we tend to bake the veg in the hero ingredients too as it's more efficient. Transfer to a large saucepan.

4. Add your hero ingredients. You can add them already cooked or roasted or else add them raw with a pinch of salt, give them a stir, put the lid back on and let them sweat for 10 to 15 minutes.

5. Add your liquid. We usually bring the liquid to the boil if we are baking our base veg, to speed up the cooking process.

6. Add your flavour agents and seasoning. Bring to the boil, then reduce the heat and simmer until all the veg are soft and cooked through.

7. Blend until smooth, then check the texture. If the texture is too thick, add a little more water and adjust the seasoning (see also Steve's top tips on texture on p. 89). Once the texture is right, taste the soup and adjust the seasoning if needed (see Steve's top tips on seasoning on p. 89).

8. Ladle the soup into warmed bowls, then scatter over your garnish and serve.

BREAKDOWN	RECIPE:	CARROT, PARSNIP AND PUMPKIN SEED	BROCCOLI, CELERIAC AND HAZELNUT	BUTTERNUT SQUASH, COCONUT AND LIME	TOMATO, CHARRED RED PEPPER AND BASIL
	BASE VEG	250g onions 250g carrots 250g celeriac 1 to 2 tbsp oil Pinch of salt	250g onions 250g carrots 250g celeriac 1 to 2 tbsp oil Pinch of salt	250g onions 250g carrots 250g celeriac 1 to 2 tbsp oil Pinch of salt	250g onions 250g carrots 250g celeriac 1 to 2 tbsp oil Pinch of salt
	HERO INGREDIENTS	300g carrots 300g parsnips 100g pumpkin seeds	350g broccoli 250g celeriac 50g hazelnuts	1kg butternut squash, peeled and roasted (p. 298)	1kg red peppers, roasted (p. 300)
	LIQUID	2.5 litres veg stock	2.5 litres veg stock	1.75 litres veg stock or water 800ml coconut milk	2 × 400g tins of chopped tomatoes 1.75 litres veg stock or water
	FLAVOUR AGENTS AND SEASONING	2 tbsp tamari or soy sauce 2 tsp salt 1 tsp ground cumin ½ tsp ground black pepper	Juice of ½ a lemon 2 tsp salt ½ tsp ground black pepper	2 tsp salt ½ tsp ground black pepper Zest and juice of 1 lime	1 small bunch of fresh basil, chopped 2 tsp salt ½ tsp ground black pepper
	GARNISH	Toasted pumpkin seeds (p. 301)	Roughly chopped hazelnuts	Lime zest Coconut yoghurt	Basil leaves

MORE SMOOTH SOUP VARIATIONS

1. Follow the instructions on p. 80.

2. Point to note: When making soups with dried lentils you will have to add more water because they soak up more liquid, which is why the Indian golden lentil and carrot soup calls for 3 litres of stock.

RECIPE:	INDIAN GOLDEN LENTIL AND CARROT	CREAM OF MUSHROOM	SUN-DRIED TOMATO AND ROASTED GARLIC	CARROT, GINGER AND TURMERIC
BASE VEG	250g onions 250g carrots 250g celeriac 1 to 2 tbsp oil Pinch of salt	350g onions 350g celeriac 1 to 2 tbsp oil Pinch of salt	250g onions 250g carrots 250g celeriac 1 to 2 tbsp oil Pinch of salt	250g onions 250g carrots 250g celeriac 1 to 2 tbsp oil Pinch of salt
HERO INGREDIENTS	300g carrots 100g split red lentils	400g mushrooms 150g cashew nuts	100g sun-dried tomatoes 1 head of roasted garlic (p. 298)	500g carrots 250g celeriac 25g fresh ginger
LIQUID	3 litres veg stock (see point 2 opposite)	2.5 litres veg stock	2 × 400g tins of chopped tomatoes 1.7 litres veg stock	2.5 litres veg stock
FLAVOUR AGENTS AND SEASONING	2 tbsp curry powder 2 tbsp tamari or soy sauce 2 tsp salt 1 tsp ground cumin ¾ tsp ground turmeric ½ tsp ground black pepper	1½ tsp salt ½ tsp ground black pepper 3 tbsp nutritional yeast 2 tbsp tamari or soy sauce	1½ tbsp maple syrup 1 tbsp tamari or soy sauce 1 tsp salt ½ tsp ground black pepper ½ tsp chilli powder	2 tsp salt 1½ tsp ground turmeric ½ tsp ground black pepper Pinch of ground cinnamon
GARNISH	Sliced red chilli Coriander leaves	Chopped spring onions Cracked pepper	Flaked almonds	Chilli flakes Lime zest

BREAKDOWN ↑ ↓

CHUNKY SOUP

We love a good, wholesome, chunky soup, particularly one that walks the line between a soup and a stew, which one might even call a stoup!

When making a chunky soup, you need to chop all your base veg and hero ingredients into bite-size pieces since the soup won't be blended. This means that a chunky soup will usually take a little longer to cook than a smooth one.

We almost always use a combination of some sort of pulse/legume (bean/lentil) and veg, as if it's just veg it ends up being too starchy and doesn't have enough substance to it. If you're using dried lentils or beans in a chunky soup, their dry weight won't make up the standard 20% of the volume of your hero ingredients in your soup. Dried lentils or beans will usually expand to up to five times their dry weight when cooked, so, for example, if you use 200g of dried red lentils, these will become approx. 1kg once cooked. The same goes for adding rice to your soups – dried rice will expand to three times its weight in terms of volume, so, for example, 100g of brown basmati rice will be 300g once it's cooked.

We love to add greens to chunky soups just before serving. They wilt in the heat and give a sense of freshness that lifts the appearance of a soup. Adding a good handful of baby spinach, chopped young kale or even a bunch of chopped fresh herbs will take your chunky soup to the next level.

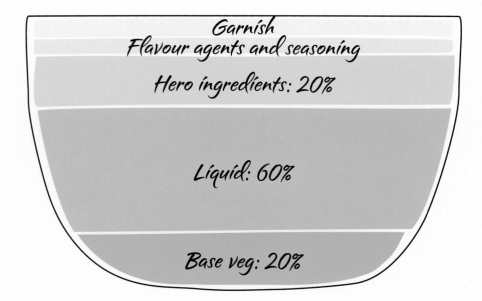

Garnish
Flavour agents and seasoning
Hero ingredients: 20%
Liquid: 60%
Base veg: 20%

Makes 4 litres (8 x 500ml servings)

We base our chunky soup framework around a 4-litre pot of soup, which will give you 8 × 500ml servings.

1. Peel and roughly chop your base veg and hero ingredients into bite-size pieces. Drain and rinse the beans or chickpeas (if using).

2. Heat the oil in a large saucepan on a high heat. Add the base veg to the pan and cook, stirring, for a couple of minutes. Reduce the heat to medium, add a good pinch of salt, then put a lid on the pan and cook for a further 10 minutes, stirring occasionally. The veg will essentially steam in their own juices, making them soft, tender and succulent.

3. Add the hero ingredients and cook for a further 3 to 4 minutes.

4. Add the liquid and the flavouring agents and seasoning. Bring to the boil, then reduce the heat and simmer for 20 minutes, until everything is soft and cooked through.

5. Check the texture. If the texture is too thick, add a little more water and adjust the seasoning (see Steve's top tips on texture on p. 89). Once the texture is right, taste the soup and adjust the seasoning if needed (see Steve's top tips on seasoning on p. 89).

6. Ladle the soup into warmed bowls, then scatter over your garnish and serve.

RECIPE:	SPANISH LENTIL AND TOMATO	INDIAN RED LENTIL AND COCONUT	SWEET POTATO, WHITE BEAN AND FENNEL	MOROCCAN AUBERGINE, CHICKPEA AND TOMATO
BASE VEG	250g onion 250g carrot 250g celeriac 1 to 2 tbsp oil Pinch of salt	250g onion 250g carrot 250g potato 1 to 2 tbsp oil Pinch of salt	250g onion 250g carrot 250g fennel 1 to 2 tbsp oil Pinch of salt	250g onion 250g carrot 250g celeriac 1 to 2 tbsp oil Pinch of salt
HERO INGREDIENTS	100g dried brown, green or Puy lentils	150g dried split red lentils	1 × 400g tin of butter beans 400g sweet potato	1 × 400g tin of chickpeas 400g aubergine
LIQUID	2 × 400g tins of chopped tomatoes 1.4 litres veg stock	1 × 400g tin of chopped tomatoes 1 litre veg stock 800ml coconut milk	2.2 litres veg stock	1 × 400g tin of chopped tomatoes 1.8 litres veg stock or water
FLAVOUR AGENTS AND SEASONING	3 tbsp tamari or soy sauce 2 tsp paprika ½ tsp smoked paprika ½ tsp ground black pepper	2 tbsp tamari or soy sauce 1½ tbsp curry powder 2 tsp paprika 2 tsp ground cumin ½ tsp ground black pepper	2 bay leaves 2 tsp salt ½ tsp black pepper	2 tsp paprika 2 tsp salt ½ tsp ground cinnamon ½ tsp chilli powder ½ tsp ground black pepper
GARNISH	50g baby spinach	Chopped fresh coriander Flaked almonds	Fennel leaves	Chopped fresh coriander Drizzle of coconut yoghurt Chopped pistachios Sesame seeds

BREAKDOWN →
← BREAKDOWN

STEVE'S TIPS FOR TURNING A GOOD SOUP INTO A GREAT SOUP

Colour

The colour of a soup will affect people's perceptions of it, particularly if the end consumers are kids! We've found that soups are always more popular if they have a strong, clear colour, so try to have a good idea of what colour you want your soup to be. Otherwise, if you just blend lots of different veg together, the soup can end up a watery, greeny-yellowy colour, which can be off-putting even if the soup tastes great.

The hero ingredients will be one of the main determinants of the colour of your soup. In addition to your base veg, the following hero ingredients will have the following effects on the colour of your soup:

- Potato, celeriac, parsnip and/or cauliflower: White

- Carrots: Orange

- Sweet potato, butternut squash and/or pumpkin: Yellow-orange

- Leeks: Typically a light shade of green

- Spinach and other greens: Green, but once cooked for longer than 10 minutes they start to lose their bright, vibrant colour

- Broccoli: Green or greenish-yellow once cooked

- Beetroot: Vibrant purple

Strong-coloured spices can also affect the colour of your soup:

- Paprika (but you'd need to use quite a lot): Red

- Turmeric: Yellow

- Curry powder: A dirty yellow

Another point to note: if you're making a white soup, don't add carrots or any other bright-coloured veg to your base veg or hero ingredients. Use white vegetables only, such as onions, celeriac, parsnip, cauliflower, etc.

Texture

For a smooth soup, you want a creamy texture that coats your mouth. For a chunky soup, you want it to have a well-seasoned stock and tender veg.

If your soup is too thick, heavy or gloopy, add more liquid (water or veg stock). Start by adding a little liquid at a time until you reach the desired texture. However, by adding more liquid you will also be diluting the flavour of the soup, so you will probably have to adjust the seasoning too. Taste it and see if it needs more salt, or would tamari or soy sauce carry the flavour better? Once you have achieved a good balance with salt, then look to the other seasonings – does it need more spice? Or maybe a little acid, such as a squeeze of lemon or lime juice?

If your soup is too thin, add some more cooked veg, tinned beans, etc. to help bulk it up. If it's a smooth soup, you will have to blend them through it again. Some good foods to bulk up your soup are:

- Tinned beans of any type (just drain and rinse them first)
- Cooked potatoes or other starchy veg, such as sweet potato, pumpkin or celeriac
- Any cooked veg that fits with the soup you're making

Start by adding a little at a time until you reach your desired texture, then adjust the seasoning as outlined above.

Taste

Taste is the most central aspect to soup success and it ultimately boils down to seasoning. As mentioned in the texture section above, you want to start with salt to try to achieve harmony. In terms of salt, you have two main options: salt or umami. We normally go for umami, as it has an extra dimension. Start with a little tamari or soy sauce, unless your soup is meant to be white, in which case just use salt. If it's a coloured soup, the tamari or soy sauce will make the colour slightly darker.

Sweet, bitter and acid are the other elements of seasoning. Added sweetness is often not required in a soup, as the base veg usually provide enough. Bitterness is normally not a desired taste in soups either, so it's best to avoid that too. Acid is used to cut through a soup that might be too rich or too cloying, or else to add a burst of vibrancy. Start with a little at a time until you reach your desired balance. When adding acid we try to match the acid to the geographic origin of the soup. So for example if we're making an Italian white bean and fennel soup, we might use lemon juice or balsamic vinegar; if we're making a Mexican black bean soup we'll use lime juice; rice vinegar is a good match for a Japanese miso soup; or try a red wine vinegar in a French soup.

Salad

Salad traditionally used to be a green salad with some veg on top and a dressing, but now there are infinite variations and combinations. We've divided our salads into three main categories – green salads; grain, bean and cooked veg salads; and bean salads – and have included three basic dressings and three oil-free dressings so that you can mix and match.

DRESSING

Dressing is the real point of difference when it comes to salads. A good dressing should be well balanced in terms of sweetness and acid/sourness. When making your own dressing, you will need to learn the ratio of sweet to sour that you like best.

THE ESSENTIALS

Salad dressings all start with the most basic of vinaigrettes: the classic two-ingredient oil and vinegar (with a pinch of salt and pepper). Oil and vinegar are not a stable emulsion – a vinaigrette will continually want to return to its separate components – so it will need to be mixed together again just before serving. The ratio of oil to vinegar in a vinaigrette is typically three parts oil to one part vinegar (3:1).

(Lemon, lime, orange or grapefruit juices lend a lovely brightness when subbed in for a portion of the vinegar in a vinaigrette. But as the name indicates, this dressing has to include only vinegar to be considered a true vinaigrette.)

Oil: Very often the more expensive the oil, such as a cold-pressed organic extra virgin olive oil or sunflower oil, the stronger, sharper and more acidic the taste. An inexpensive, basic olive oil or sunflower oil will typically have a more neutral flavour. Taste your oil to get an understanding of what you like. If it's too powerful for your palate, dilute it with a little neutral-tasting oil.

The main oils we use in our salad dressings are olive, sunflower and rapeseed oil. Rapeseed oil is generally more nutty in flavour, with a golden colour. It's also higher in omega-3 fatty acids and lower in saturated fat than olive or sunflower oil.

Mustard: Whisk a little mustard into your vinaigrette and watch emulsification magic happen to form a smooth, creamy and more stable dressing.

Sweetness: The key to a tasty vinaigrette is striking the right balance between the levels of acid and fat. Incorporating a sweetener like maple or date syrup or molasses can soften the acidity of the vinegar. A little sweetener goes a long way, so start with ½ to 1 teaspoon of liquid sweetener per 150ml vinaigrette.

Garlic and shallots: Garlic and shallots work well with oil and vinegar and add another dimension to your dressing. Add a finely chopped clove of garlic or a spoonful of minced shallot to your dressing (or blend the dressing in a blender). If the taste of raw garlic is too intense for you, try adding a roasted clove (see p. 298) or a pinch of garlic powder. To tame the oniony flavour of raw shallot, soak it in the vinegar for 5 to 15 minutes before adding the rest of the ingredients. The only downside to adding either of these to your dressing is that the shelf life will be reduced.

Herbs: Fresh or dried herbs make vinaigrettes shine. Try any herb (or mix of herbs) that you have on hand: basil, thyme, parsley, dill, oregano, mint, tarragon, rosemary, coriander and chives are all great choices. You'll need about ½ teaspoon dried or 1 tablespoon fresh chopped herbs per tablespoon of vinegar, but you can always add more to taste. Thyme and rosemary (the more hardy fresh herbs) tend to be used most often in dressings. However, just like adding garlic or shallot to a dressing, by adding fresh herbs the shelf life will be reduced.

Spices: Enliven your vinaigrette with toasted, crushed or ground spices such as chilli flakes, cumin seeds, coriander seeds, fennel seeds, poppy seeds or smoked or sweet paprika. You can also add some garlic and/or onion powder, which works well too and won't shorten the shelf life. Start by adding ¼ teaspoon of spice per tablespoon of vinegar. These flavour additions are especially nice with grain or lentil salads, grilled or roasted vegetables or in marinades. Grated fresh ginger adds an extra dimension and we tend to blend it through Asian-style dressings along with tamari or soy sauce, lime juice and maple syrup.

Extras: There are lots of additional flavour agents that you can add to give depth and a certain je ne sais quoi to your dressing. Here are a few that we use regularly:

- **Miso:** Add 1 teaspoon of miso to each tablespoon of vinegar to add a distinctive umami boost. If you're using miso in combination with salt, you will need less salt, as miso contains sodium too. You will need to mix or blend it well to incorporate it fully into the dressing.

- **Vegan mayonnaise:** Vegan mayo (p. 320) will add richness and more body to your dressing. This type of dressing goes well with coleslaw or grated root veg. We use vegan mayo in place of oil, as one of the main ingredients in mayo is oil, so the ratio of vegan mayo to vinegar/citrus is the same as a regular vinaigrette: three parts vegan mayo to one part vinegar/citrus (3:1).

- **Tamari or soy sauce:** Either of these adds that umami boost and works great in Asian-style dressings. We love to blend them with sesame oil, lime juice, rice wine vinegar, maple syrup, fresh ginger and garlic.

- **Nuts and nut butters:** These will give body and richness to your dressings. We tend to replace most of the oil with nuts/nut butter in a ratio of two parts nuts/nut butter to one part oil (2:1) and blend until smooth. In other words, the base framework when using nuts/nut butters in a dressing is two parts nuts/nut butter to one part oil and one part vinegar (2:1:1). You will need to blend your dressing in a high-speed blender when using nuts/nut butter in dressings to get a smooth texture.

- **Fruit and veg:** For example, adding some fresh cherry tomatoes will give your dressing a tomato flavour.

- **Nutritional yeast:** This can add a cheesy note to your dressings, but just make sure that you actually like nutritional yeast before using it, as it can be a love/hate taste for some people! A little goes a long way, so start with a good pinch per tablespoon of vinegar, taste and adjust accordingly.

Dressing pointers

Regardless of how creative you get with your vinaigrette, a few standard rules apply:

1. You can either make only a little at a time (just what you need for one meal or salad) or make a lot – a vinaigrette will keep for 3 days or longer in the fridge, depending on the shelf life of the ingredients you choose. The fresh ingredients, such as fresh herbs, alliums (garlic, shallots, chives, etc.) and citrus juices, are what shorten the shelf life. You can store your vinaigrette at room temperature for months if no fresh ingredients are included.

2. Dressing your salad will reduce its shelf life. If you want your salad to last longer or if you're making it ahead of time, assemble it without the dressing, then dress it just before serving.

3. Vinaigrettes aren't just for lettuce! They can also be a great marinade for veg, tofu and tempeh. Or serve your vinaigrette with bread for dipping, drizzle it over sliced fresh tomatoes, use it as a sauce for steamed artichokes or toss with roasted or grilled vegetables, such as asparagus, potatoes, aubergines and butternut squash.

4. Season carefully. Taste for salt, pepper, sweet and sour. Before you dress the whole salad (the point of no return), dip one leaf into the dressing, taste and adjust the seasoning if needed.

5. If you're using raw garlic in a dressing, it's best to crush it to a paste with a little salt – this breaks it down more than a garlic crusher can. The flavour will spread more evenly through the dressing, with no little lumps of raw garlic.

BASIC DRESSINGS

Just like salad combinations, there is no end to the possibilities when it comes to all the varieties of dressings you can make. Armed with the essential ingredients and dressing pointers on the previous pages and this recipe framework, you can make your own amazing and creative salad dressings.

BREAKDOWN →	RECIPE:	BASIC MUSTARD VINAIGRETTE	FANCIER VINAIGRETTE	ASIAN GARLIC AND GINGER FLAVOUR BOMB
	OIL	100ml olive oil	100ml rapeseed oil	100ml olive oil
	VINEGAR	35ml apple cider vinegar	35ml balsamic vinegar	Juice of 1 lemon
	MUSTARD	¾ tbsp Dijon mustard	1 tbsp Dijon mustard	
	SWEETENER		1 tsp maple syrup	2 tbsp maple syrup
	FLAVOUR AGENTS AND SEASONING	¼ tsp salt Freshly ground black pepper	4 sprigs of fresh thyme ½ tsp garlic powder ¼ tsp salt Freshly ground black pepper	3 garlic cloves ½ a fresh red chilli 1 × 2cm piece of ginger 5 tbsp tamari or soy sauce

→

1. To prepare the flavour agents, strip the thyme leaves from their stalks if you're making the fancier vinaigrette. If you're making the Asian garlic and ginger flavour bomb, peel and crush the garlic. Deseed and finely chop the chilli. Peel and finely chop the ginger.

2. Put all the ingredients into a blender and mix until well combined. The Asian dressing will need to be blended for a little longer.

3. The fancier vinaigrette and the Asian dressing will keep in a sealed jar in the fridge for 3 days, but the basic mustard vinaigrette will last for up to 1 month in the fridge.

OIL-FREE DRESSINGS

Makes 120ml to 200ml

All the recipes on our four-week online Happy Heart Course are oil-free, including the salad dressings. As a result, we've been making oil-free dressings for more than eight years now and have been tweaking them as we go along.

We use fruit juice instead of oil more often than not, which means these dressings aren't as thick and heavy as oil-based ones. We usually add plenty of additional flavour agents, sweeteners and other herbs or spices to add more flavour and make up for the lack of oil.

1. Simply put all the ingredients into a bowl and whisk to combine, or blend in a blender for a really smooth dressing.

2. These oil-free dressings don't store as well as an oil-based vinaigrette (with no fresh ingredients) and typically only keep for around 3 days in a sealed jar in the fridge.

RECIPE:	TANGY LEMON MUSTARD DRESSING	SMOKY BBQ DRESSING	ITALIAN DRESSING
JUICE	60ml lemon juice 60ml apple juice	2 tsp lemon juice	
VINEGAR		60ml apple cider vinegar	60ml rice wine vinegar
WATER	30ml water	30ml water	30ml water
MUSTARD	2½ tsp Dijon mustard	1 tsp Dijon mustard	1 tsp Dijon mustard
SWEETENER	½ tbsp maple syrup	3 tbsp maple syrup	1 tbsp maple syrup
FLAVOUR AGENTS AND SEASONING	1 garlic clove, peeled and crushed Zest of 1 lemon ¼ tsp salt Pinch of freshly ground black pepper	1 tsp onion powder ½ tsp garlic powder ½ tsp smoked paprika Salt and freshly ground black pepper	1 tbsp nutritional yeast ½ tsp garlic powder ½ tsp dried oregano ½ tsp dried basil ¼ tsp salt Pinch of freshly ground black pepper

BREAKDOWN

GREEN SALADS

Green salads are made up of three main components – leaves and lettuce, veg and fruit toppings, and dressing – as well as an optional garnish that you can customize however you like using the lists below and your own imagination, or use the framework on p. 105 if you need a little more inspiration.

THE ESSENTIALS

Leaves and lettuce: Start with a bed of leaves or lettuce. When we were growing up, that meant iceberg or butterhead lettuce, but there are so many other options now. Experiment until you find the combinations and flavours you like the best, but here are a few of our favourite base leaves and lettuces:

- Rocket
- Baby spinach
- Mizuna (a light, neutral-tasting, stringy green)
- Mesclun (a mix of coloured baby leaves)
- Watercress (quite bitter and dominant)
- Baby mustard greens (quite bitter and spicy)
- Baby chard leaves
- Radicchio
- Oak leaf lettuce
- Romaine/cos lettuce
- Baby gem lettuce
- Batavia lettuce

Toppings: The toppings add flavour, colour, moisture and a variety of textures to your salad. We love including fruit in our green salads, particularly when it's a main meal, as it adds a little sweetness, juice and pops of colour. We all eat with our eyes first and a good mix of colour really sets a salad alight.

Veg toppings:

- Sliced tomatoes
- Halved cherry tomatoes

- Thinly sliced red onions or pickled red onions
- Cucumber slices
- Sliced spring onions
- Sliced radishes
- Tinned or cooked beans/chickpeas
- Green beans
- Mangetout
- Sugar snap peas
- Sliced red peppers
- Grated carrots
- Sprouts (microgreens)
- Chopped fresh herbs

Fruit toppings:

- Raspberries
- Blueberries
- Orange segments
- Grapefruit segments
- Pomegranate seeds
- Peaches or nectarines, sliced
- Apricots, sliced, halved or quartered
- Bite-size pieces of watermelon
- Sliced ripe avocado
- Black Kalamata olives (yes, avocados and olives are technically fruit!)
- Capers (again, they're a fruit that is salty, acidic and juicy)

Dressing: You can use any of the dressings on pp. 96–9 or whatever your favourite dressing is.

Garnish: Optional extras like toasted nuts or seeds (or a mix such as gomashio, za'atar or dukkah, see p. 310) or fresh herbs will add a final flourish.

GREEN SALAD

Serves 2

The green salads in this framework are substantial enough to have as a main meal (rather than a side) that will leave you feeling light, nourished and happy.

1. Wash and dry your greens/leaves in a salad spinner, then transfer them to a large bowl. Drizzle over the dressing, then gently toss, making sure all the leaves are lightly coated. Divide between two wide, shallow serving bowls.

2. Add your veg toppings, starting with the green veg first and layering the more colourful veg on top, spreading them out evenly across the greens/leaves. Then layer on your fruit toppings to make your salad really pretty. If you're using grapefruit and orange segments, be sure to squeeze over any leftover juice too.

3. Taste and adjust the seasoning to your palate – it might need a pinch of salt, some acid or a little dusting of chilli flakes.

4. Sprinkle over the garnish, and serve straight away.

RECIPE:	BERRYLICIOUS SALAD	AVOCADO AND CITRUS SALAD	POMEGRANATE AND WHITE PEACH SALAD	BLUEBERRY AND WATERMELON SALAD
GREENS/ LEAVES	100g to 150g mixed leaves, such as rocket, baby spinach, baby gem, etc.	100g mixture of oak leaf and cos lettuce leaves	100g leaves of choice	100g leaves of choice
DRESSING	2 to 4 tbsp basic mustard vinaigrette (p. 96)	2 to 4 tbsp of any dressing from pp. 96–9	2 to 4 tbsp basic mustard vinaigrette (p. 96)	2 to 4 tbsp of any dressing from pp. 96–9
VEG TOPPINGS	200g mix of sliced spring onions, diced cucumber and halved cherry tomatoes	200g mix of avocado slices, black olives and sliced artichoke hearts from a jar	20g pickled fennel (p. 308)	200g mix of multicoloured halved cherry tomatoes, grated carrots and beetroot, and sliced sugar snap peas
FRUIT TOPPINGS	200g mix of fresh raspberries and halved strawberries	Segments from 1 medium orange and 1 grapefruit	200g mix of pomegranate seeds and white peach wedges	200g mix of fresh blueberries and watermelon chunks
GARNISH	40g toasted pumpkin, sunflower and/ or sesame seeds (p. 301) Small handful of beet sprouts (optional)	30g dukkah (p. 310)	75g toasted pine nuts (p. 301)	30g gomashio (p. 310) 5g fresh mint leaves

BREAKDOWN

GRAIN, BEAN AND COOKED VEG SALADS

We love hearty, substantial salads of beans, grains and cooked veg. They are usually served cold and walk the line between a salad and a side dish, but they can also be a meal in and of themselves. You can use the following framework to make sure you get a satisfying mix of greens, grains, beans and toppings with a good variety of ingredients.

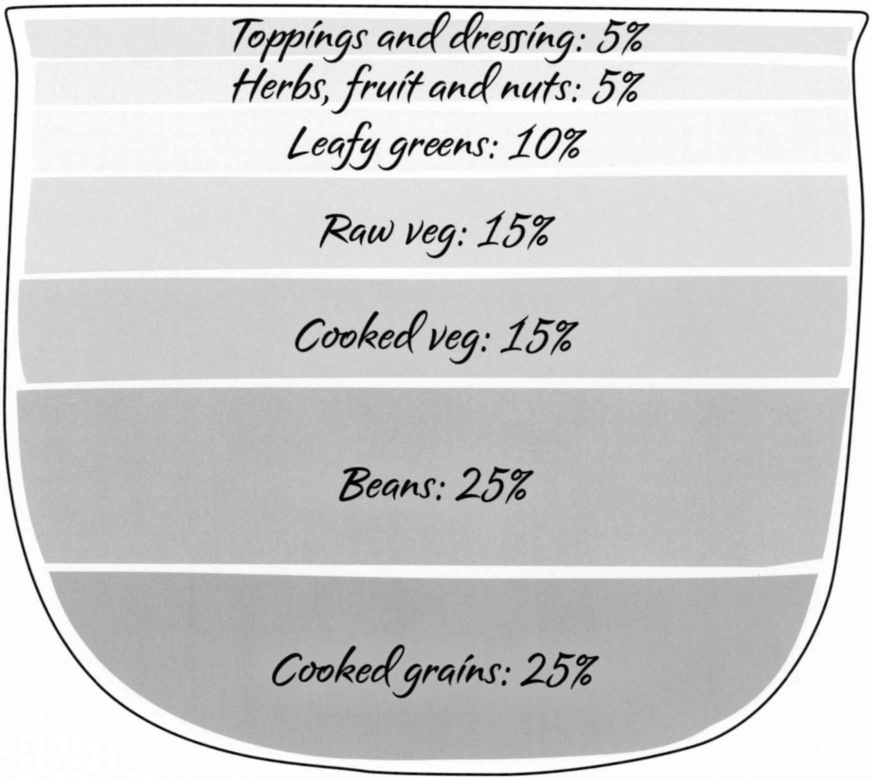

Toppings and dressing: 5%

Herbs, fruit and nuts: 5%

Leafy greens: 10%

Raw veg: 15%

Cooked veg: 15%

Beans: 25%

Cooked grains: 25%

$\rightarrow$

Serves 2 to 4

1. When cooking your grain, make sure to add some salt as you cook it. That way the salt cooks into the grain as opposed to if you season it later, when it simply sits on the surface.

2. If you're making the Moroccan quinoa and smoky pepper salad, add 1 teaspoon of ground turmeric to make it yellow. If you're making the Italian pumpkin and red rice salad but can't find red rice, use brown rice instead and add 2 tablespoons of sweet paprika and 1 teaspoon of oil to it. If you're making the easy noodle salad, cook the noodles according to the packet instructions.

3. Drain and rinse the beans. Peel and cut your raw veg. Finely chop the fresh herbs, including the stalks (with the exception of herbs with harder stalks, such as mint, rosemary, thyme and sage).

4. To make the dressing, deseed and finely dice the chilli and peel and grate the ginger (if using). Whisk or blend all the dressing ingredients together.

5. Now think about presentation. In a large serving bowl, start with the cooked grain, then add the beans and raw veg. Drizzle over the dressing, then add the cooked veg, leafy greens and herbs and gently mix through. Add the seasoning, then taste and adjust if needed. Finally, scatter over the garnish (if using), and serve.

RECIPE:	TABBOULEH CHICKPEA SALAD	MOROCCAN QUINOA AND SMOKY PEPPER SALAD	MEXICAN RICE, BEAN AND GUACAMOLE SALAD	ITALIAN PUMPKIN AND RED RICE SALAD	EASY NOODLE SALAD
COOKED GRAIN	250g cooked bulghur wheat (p. 301)	250g cooked quinoa (p. 301) 1 tsp ground turmeric	250g cooked brown rice (p. 301)	250g cooked red rice (p. 301)	250g cooked wholewheat noodles (5 nests)
BEANS	1 × 400g tin of chickpeas	1 × 400g tin of lentils	1 × 400g tin of black beans	1 × 400g tin of butter beans	250g frozen peas, thawed
RAW VEG	100g cherry tomatoes, halved 50g spring onions, thinly sliced 50g cucumber, diced	1 red onion, thinly sliced into half-moons 50g cherry tomatoes, quartered	50g cherry tomatoes, quartered 1 bunch of spring onions, thinly sliced 2 avocados, peeled, stoned and cut into chunks 1 fresh red chilli, deseeded and thinly sliced	3 ripe tomatoes, chopped into bite-size pieces Pickled red onions (p. 308)	1 bunch of spring onions, thinly sliced 1 bunch of radishes, thinly sliced
COOKED VEG	150g roasted aubergines, chopped into bite-sized pieces (p. 298)	150g roasted peppers (p. 300) 1 tsp smoked paprika, mixed through the roasted peppers	100g roasted sweet potato, chopped into bite-sized pieces (p. 300) 50g blanched fine beans	150g roasted unpeeled pumpkin, cut into wedges (p. 300)	200g pan-fried mushrooms (p. 300)

BREAKDOWN ↑ ↓

RECIPES AND BREAKDOWN CONTINUE ON OPPOSITE PAGE

RECIPE: *CONTINUED*	TABBOULEH CHICKPEA SALAD	MOROCCAN QUINOA AND SMOKY PEPPER SALAD	MEXICAN RICE, BEAN AND GUACAMOLE SALAD	ITALIAN PUMPKIN AND RED RICE SALAD	EASY NOODLE SALAD
DRESSING	50ml olive oil Juice of 1 lemon 1 tbsp tamari or soy sauce	50ml olive oil 3 tbsp apple cider or balsamic vinegar	50ml olive oil Juice of 2 limes 2 tbsp tamari or soy sauce 1 tbsp maple syrup	50ml olive oil 2 tbsp balsamic vinegar 2 tbsp tamari or soy sauce 1 tbsp maple syrup	½ fresh red chilli ½ thumb-size piece of fresh ginger Juice of ½ lemon or 1 lime 50ml olive oil 3 tbsp tamari or soy sauce 1 tbsp maple syrup
LEAFY GREENS	100g rocket	100g baby spinach	50g rocket	100g rocket	100g baby spinach
HERBS	1 large bunch of fresh flat-leaf parsley 1 bunch of fresh mint	1 small bunch of fresh coriander	1 small bunch of fresh coriander	1 small bunch of fresh flat-leaf parsley	1 small bunch of fresh coriander
SEASONING	Salt and freshly ground black pepper	Salt and freshly ground black pepper	Pinch of salt	1 tbsp dried oregano 1 tsp dried thyme Pinch of salt	30g za'atar (p. 310)
GARNISH		4 tbsp dukkah (p.310)		50g toasted pine nuts (p. 301)	Pomegranate seeds

BREAKDOWN CONTINUED ↑ ↓

BEAN SALADS

When we make bean salads in our cafés we cook dried beans from scratch, since we are making such large quantities, but when we make bean salads at home we always use tinned beans for ease and practicality. If you'd rather cook your own beans than use tinned, see the instructions on p. 302. The basic framework for a bean salad is:

Leafy greens, herbs and dressing: 20%

Raw veg: 20%

Cooked veg: 20%

Cooked or tinned beans: 40%

Plain cooked beans aren't the tastiest thing ever, so your dressing and veg are really important elements of a good bean salad. A nice bit of acidity and salt with a generous serving of oil makes all the difference too.

You need a strong, 'all singing, all dancing' type of dressing when it comes to bean salads. You also need a dressing with more body than a typical vinaigrette, one that will stick to the beans and not simply pool at the bottom of the bowl. As a result, we tend to use thicker dressings, such as pesto, salsa or vegan mayonnaise, in bean salads. We also like to use the following veg:

- Roasted squash and sweet potato both have vibrant colours that help a bean salad to pop.

- Roasted root veg, especially a nice assortment of carrot, beetroot, parsnip and celeriac, can be lovely and colourful.

- Leeks are one of our favourite veg but are often forgotten. Succulent roasted leeks are hard to beat, as they're sweet, savoury and juicy all at the same time. We use the full leek, including the green part.

- Red onion is a nice one for colour. We will usually roast them on their own or as part of a roasted veg mix. Pickled red onions (see p. 308) also work well.

- Roasted or grilled Mediterranean veg, such as courgettes, aubergines, peppers and fennel, are always good.

- See the list on pp. 100–101 of the green salad section for ideas for raw veg.

Serves 2 to 4

1. Drain and rinse the beans. Finely chop the fresh herbs, including the stalks (with the exception of herbs with harder stalks, such as mint, rosemary, thyme and sage).

2. To make the dressing, simply whisk or blend all the dressing ingredients together.

3. Put all the ingredients into a large bowl and mix well. Taste and adjust the seasoning if needed.

4. Bean salads will typically keep for up to 3 days in the fridge, even after being dressed (unlike a green salad), so they're ideal for making ahead of time for lunch or a meal on the go. We usually add a squeeze of lemon or lime or a drizzle of oil to freshen up a bean salad if we're eating it on day 2 or day 3.

5. If serving a bean salad from the fridge, take it out an hour before serving, as you can always taste more when it's at room temperature versus when it's cold.

BREAKDOWN ↑↓	RECIPE:	RED PEPPER PESTO AND BEAN SALAD	CANARY ISLAND MOJO BEAN SALAD	LENTIL AND PUMPKIN SALAD
	BEANS	1 × 400g tin of butter beans 1 × 400g tin of chickpeas	2 × 400g tins of black beans	2 × 400g tins of lentils
	COOKED VEG	200g roasted leeks (p. 300)	1 roasted red pepper (p. 300) 1 roasted yellow pepper (p. 300)	200g roasted pumpkin (p. 300)
	RAW VEG	100g cherry tomatoes, quartered 1 bunch of spring onions, finely chopped	1 red onion, peeled and finely diced ½ cucumber, chopped into cubes	3 ripe tomatoes, chopped into chunks
	DRESSING	160ml roasted red pepper pesto (p. 167) 50ml olive oil	160ml coriander pesto (p. 167) 50ml olive oil	Juice of 1 lime 100ml olive oil 2 tbsp tamari or soy sauce 1 tbsp maple syrup 1 tsp salt
	LEAFY GREENS	100g rocket	50g baby spinach	100g rocket
	HERBS	A few sprigs of fresh basil	A few sprigs of fresh coriander	30g fresh flat-leaf parsley
	ACID	Juice of 1 lemon	Juice of 1 lemon	
	SEASONING	Pinch of salt	1 tsp salt	Pinch of salt

HOW TO MAKE YOUR SALAD MORE INTERESTING

People can often think that salads are bland and one-dimensional, so here are a few tips to inject more variety and flavour.

Cut your veg in a more interesting way

It's amazing how simply changing the shape of your chopped veg can make your salad suddenly look a whole lot more interesting. Here are some different cuts to add more variety.

- **Knife cuts:** Instead of slicing straight through your veg at a 90° angle, cut it at a 45° angle instead.

- **Peeler:** Use a peeler to make long strips of carrot, courgette and cucumber that can be rolled up or even pickled (see p. 307).

- **Mandoline:** Try using a mandoline to get finer cuts on cucumbers, fennel, beans, peppers, carrots and radishes and turn them into strips. Simply season with a little salt, oil and lemon to add another texture, dimension and flavour to your salads. Just be careful of your fingers!

- **Julienne:** Julienne is a fancy French word for cutting your veg into thin matchsticks. This works great with firmer veg such as carrots, peppers and green beans, as well as with deseeded cucumbers. It's not very practical to do by hand due to the amount of time it takes, but food processors often come with a julienne blade, which makes it a quick and easy job. We usually do this when making carrot, beetroot and grated root veg salads. You can also get julienne peelers if you don't have a food processor.

- **Spiralizing:** Spiralizers became popular a few years ago and are a fun way to make veg seem more multidimensional. The best veg to spiralize are courgettes, carrots and other firmer root veg.

- **Grating:** When you grate veg, it removes excess moisture. All box graters have at least two sides, so you can do a finer or a thicker grate depending on what suits your salad best. Season the grated veg well to add another layer of flavour.

Grill some veg

Use a chargrill pan, your oven grill or your barbecue to add a charred flavour and a textural contrast to a salad. Courgettes, peppers and aubergines are terrific when grilled.

- **Courgettes:** Once they're grilled, it's like the flavour and true beauty of a courgette are unlocked. Just slice a courgette into strips about 5mm thick, coat with a little oil, season with a pinch of salt and put on a hot chargrill pan until the strips soften and get some nice griddle lines, then turn and do the same on the other side.

- **Peppers:** Grill until the peppers are charring around the edges.

- **Aubergines:** Aubergines get a bad rap because people often undercook them, so they end up rubbery and chewy as opposed to soft and gooey. The key with aubergines is to cook them until they are super soft, with a melt-in-your-mouth texture.

Add a pickle

Pickling veg such as red onions, carrots and fennel is a really simple way to get a different flavour into your salads. You can make a quick pickle in as little as 10 minutes – see the recipes on p. 308. Once you learn how to pickle, you'll be delighted with yourself and your salads will never be the same!

Add a seed mix

You'll be surprised by how much a seed mix such as gomashio, dukkah or za'atar (see p. 310) can transform a salad. Use them to add more flavour and a little crunch.

Burgers

We were total jocks when we were teenagers and loved nothing more than a good burger straight from the BBQ. When we became vegan a few years later, we thought we would really miss burgers and couldn't imagine that a decent vegan burger existed, but over the years we have learned how to make a top-class burger that also just so happens to be vegan. We know that the words 'vegan' and 'burger' don't typically go together, but in our experience a good vegan burger can be hard to beat and is the perfect comfort food, particularly if you grew up eating burgers.

We have about 15 vegan burger video recipes on our YouTube channel if you're looking to try a more innovative and unusual vegan burger, including an arancini burger, a Japanese umami burger, a jackfruit 'pulled pork' burger, a jerk burger and a falafel burger. Here, though, we have stuck to the essentials and have included recipes for three types of burgers: wholefood burgers, vital wheat gluten burgers and TVP burgers. There are some really good meat alternative burgers on the market now, but they are reasonably straightforward to make at home provided you have a couple of specific ingredients. The two ingredients we have played with quite a bit are vital wheat gluten and textured vegetable protein (TVP). Both can be bought online and in many health food stores.

WHOLEFOOD BURGERS

The average burger is somewhere between 120g and 150g in weight. We usually make about 1kg of burger mix at a time, which will give you 6 to 8 burgers. We typically base our wholefood burgers around six components (with the crust being an added extra).

Crust

Flavour agents and seasoning

Binder: 5%

Fat: 10%–15%

Starch: 20%–30%

Cooked veg: 20%–30%

Beans: 25%

THE ESSENTIALS

Beans: Tinned beans bind the burger and make up quite a bit of the body of the burger too. Use whatever tinned beans you have and prefer, such as tinned chickpeas, butter beans, kidney beans, cannellini beans, etc. When using tinned beans, just make sure to drain and rinse them well, as the soaking liquid is believed to be where some of the beans' flatulent properties come from. But don't feel limited to tinned beans – if you like to soak and cook your own dried beans from scratch (see p. 302), use those instead.

Cooked veg: Certain vegetables work better than others when it comes to vegan burgers – we like to use veg that are more starchy and don't have much water content. Whatever veg you use will have to be pre-cooked. We tend to bake or fry any veg we use for burgers, as it helps to reduce the moisture content, whereas steaming or boiling actually creates more moisture and thus makes it harder for the burger to stay together. The cooked veg usually make up to 20–30% of the weight of the burger (but this is flexible). Here is a list of veg that work well in vegan burgers (see pp. 298–300 for instructions on how to cook the veg):

- Roasted sweet potatoes and regular potatoes
- Roasted butternut squash and pumpkin
- Roasted or pan-fried mushrooms (our favourites are oyster, shiitake and chestnut)
- Roasted aubergines

Starch: Starch helps to bind the burger and is always cooked first. Starch absorbs moisture, which helps the burger to stay together and maintain its structure. We usually use breadcrumbs, cooked quinoa, cooked wholemeal couscous, cooked brown rice or oat flakes as the starch element.

Fat: A conventional meat burger typically has a 15% to 20% fat content. For a wholefood burger to be as satisfying and tasty as a more traditional burger, it needs to be similarly high in fat, usually around 10% to 15%. We use wholefood sources of fat, such as nuts, seeds and nut butters, as these contain plenty of nutrition and fibre in addition to the fat. Nuts have the added bonus of giving a bit more bite and texture to your burger too.

Binder: The binder is the 'glue' that holds the burger together and helps to create a tight texture so that when you bite into it, the burger isn't so soft that it falls to pieces. The binder absorbs any excess moisture and thus holds everything together, like the way an egg binds together many cake batters.

The two binders that we typically use are a flax or chia 'egg' (see p. 303). Other binders that we have used include brown rice flour, regular plain flour, cornflour, tapioca starch, arrowroot, psyllium husk and vital wheat gluten (see p. 130 for more info on this). Start by adding 1 tablespoon of any of these and see how sticky your burger mix is, then add another tablespoon if needed until it seems tight enough that your burgers will hold their shape.

Flavour agents: We like to add 2 tablespoons of tamari or soy sauce to the burger mix to give an undertone of flavour and an umami boost that are really satisfying. We also add 2 tablespoons of lemon or lime juice or a capful of vinegar (such as apple cider or rice vinegar), but not both, as they serve the same purpose – these are all acids, which help to cut through the starch in the burger mix.

Play around with fresh or dried herbs and spices too, but be careful when using fresh herbs such as sage and rosemary, as they can be overpowering and quite divisive, a bit like olives!

- Coriander: This is one of the most popular fresh herbs, but be aware that about 10% of the population hate it, as to them it tastes like soap.

- Basil: Use sparingly, as basil isn't usually used in burgers.

- Chives: Finely chopped or snipped fresh chives add a slight onion flavour and nice flecks of green.

- Thyme: Add 1 or 2 teaspoons of fresh whole thyme leaves.

- Dried Italian herbs: Usually comprised of dried thyme, bay leaf and rosemary, this mix will add a subtle herby note to your burger.

- Smoked paprika: Can help give that smoky, beefy taste. A little goes a long way, so start with ½ teaspoon, then taste and adjust.

- Cumin seeds: Use 1 tablespoon with your veg/protein.

- Ground cumin: Will add an aromatic element to your burger, which won't suit all types of burger. Start with 1 teaspoon, then taste and adjust.

- Ground coriander: Goes well with ground cumin. Start with 1 teaspoon, then taste and adjust.

- Fennel seeds: These are a bit like Marmite – they add an aniseed flavour that people tend to either love or hate. Toast them on a hot dry pan for 5 minutes to release even more flavour. A little goes a long way, so start with ½ teaspoon, then taste and adjust.

- Chilli powder: For some extra heat and a lovely warming element, start with ½ teaspoon, then taste and adjust.

- Ground black pepper: Gives a warm, spicy kick in the back of the throat. Start with ¼ teaspoon, then taste and adjust.

For more details on flavour agents and spices, check out pp. 11–14.

Crust: Sometimes we like to coat our burger patties with something to give them more bite, more crunch or more texture contrast.

- **Chickpea/gram flour and non-dairy milk wash:** This forms a light batter on your burger to give it some textural contrast. Pour some non-dairy milk into a wide, shallow bowl and put some chickpea/gram flour into a separate wide, shallow bowl. Dip each burger in the milk, then dip it in the flour, making sure it's coated evenly all over and shaking off any excess, then add the burger straight to the hot frying pan.

- **Sesame seeds:** Coating your burger in sesame seeds will give it a lovely crunch and a distinctive look. We often do this when we make a sweet potato falafel burger, for instance. Put a mix of white and black sesame seeds on a small plate and roll the uncooked burger patties in them, giving them a nice even coating, then bake or fry them.

- **Oat or quinoa flakes:** Using a flaked grain works well to give an earthy look to your burger. It doesn't form a crust per se, like the other two options above, but adds a nice visual contrast and wholesome appeal.

- **Panko breadcrumbs:** A Japanese-style dried breadcrumb that results in an extra crispy crust. As with the chickpea flour, just dip the burgers in some non-dairy milk and then into the panko crumbs, and fry.

THE EXTRAS

The combination of the burger along with the bun (brown, white or gluten free), sauce and toppings is what will really make your burger epic. We like to use a wide range of vegan sauces and condiments: ketchup, mayo, red or green pesto, cheese, spicy salsa, hummus, sweet beet hummus, mustard, tapenade (check the index to find our recipes for these) . . . I'm sure we're forgetting some here, but you get the idea!

Your toppings offer a nice contrast of texture and can add moisture and another depth of flavour to your burger. We often use the following:

- Lettuce
- Sliced tomatoes
- Sliced avocado or guacamole (see p. 324)
- Gherkins
- Red onion rings or pickled red onions (see p. 308)
- Crimson or red sauerkraut

WHOLEFOOD BURGERS

Makes 5 to 6 burgers

Wholefood burgers don't try to mimic the texture and bite of a traditional meat burger, but rather are based around whole plant foods, making it a much healthier burger in terms of nutrition and fibre that can be just as tasty as its meat counterpart.

1. Drain and rinse the beans. Prepare the cooked veg you'll be using. If you're using quinoa, couscous or brown rice as your starch, cook them according to the packet instructions, then set aside. Finely chop the nuts if you're using them as your fat.

2. To prepare the binder, prepare the flax or chia 'eggs' as per the instructions on p. 303, then set aside.

3. In addition to your cooked veg, peel and finely chop the onions and garlic (if using).

4. Heat the oil in a medium-sized frying pan on a high heat. Add the onion, garlic and mushrooms (if using) and cook, stirring occasionally, for 3 to 4 minutes. Remove the pan from the heat and set aside.

5. In a large bowl, mash the beans and cooked veg (including the fried onion, garlic and mushrooms), using a potato masher. Add the starch, fat, binder (the 'eggs' and psyllium husks) and the flavour agents and seasoning and mix really well until thoroughly combined. The mixture should be nice and firm and easy to shape into burgers. Taste and adjust the seasoning with a little more salt, pepper or lemon juice if needed.

6. Shape into 120g to 150g burgers.

7. Heat another splash of oil in a large non-stick frying pan on a medium heat. Dip each burger into the crust ingredients, then add to the hot pan and fry for 2 to 3 minutes on each side, until nicely charred and cooked through. (Cook the burgers in batches or in two pans if necessary so that you don't crowd the pan.)

8. Alternatively, you could bake the burgers in the oven. Rub each side of the burgers lightly with oil and place on a baking tray. Bake in the oven at 180°C fan/400°F/gas 6 for 20 minutes, flipping them over halfway through.

9. Assemble the cooked burgers with whatever buns, sauces and toppings you like – and don't forget the fries on p. 139!

RECIPE:	BASIC BURGER	HIGH-PROTEIN BURGER	15-MINUTE BURGER
BEANS	1 × 400g tin of beans (any kind)	1 × 400g tin of black beans	1 × 400g tin of kidney beans or black beans
COOKED VEG	300g cooked starchy veg (see the list on p. 122) 2 tbsp oil	200g roasted sweet potato (p. 300) 2 red onions 2 garlic cloves 2 tbsp oil	1 red onion 2 garlic cloves 150g pan-fried mushrooms of choice (p. 300) 2 tbsp oil
STARCH	150g cooked wholemeal couscous (p. 301)	300g cooked quinoa (p. 301)	100g fresh breadcrumbs or cooked wholemeal couscous (p. 301)
FAT	100g toasted nuts or seeds	100g cashew nuts	3 tbsp oil
BINDER	2 flax 'eggs' (p. 303) 2 tbsp psyllium husks	2 flax 'eggs' (p. 303) 2 tbsp psyllium husks	2 chia 'eggs' (p. 303) 2 tbsp psyllium husks
FLAVOUR AGENTS AND SEASONING	2 tbsp tamari or soy sauce 2 tbsp lemon/lime juice or vinegar ½ tsp to 2 tsp spices (see list on p. 123) 1 small bunch of fresh herbs, chopped 1 tsp salt	1 small bunch of fresh coriander, chopped Juice of 1 lemon 2 tbsp tamari or soy sauce 1 tbsp cumin seeds 1 tsp salt ½ tsp freshly ground black pepper	3 tbsp tamari or soy sauce 2 tbsp nutritional yeast
CRUST	Sesame seeds (see p. 124)	Panko breadcrumbs (see p. 124)	Chickpea/gram flour and non-dairy milk wash (see p. 124)

BREAKDOWN

VITAL WHEAT GLUTEN BURGERS

Vital wheat gluten is also known as wheat protein, as it's pretty much the protein from wheat, which consists exclusively of gluten. It's a highly processed ingredient and is available online and from most health food stores. Seitan, aka 'wheat meat', is also made from vital wheat gluten. We came across vital wheat gluten a few years back and found it to be really useful in creating meat substitutes, including vegan steak!

Vital wheat gluten burgers use the following framework:

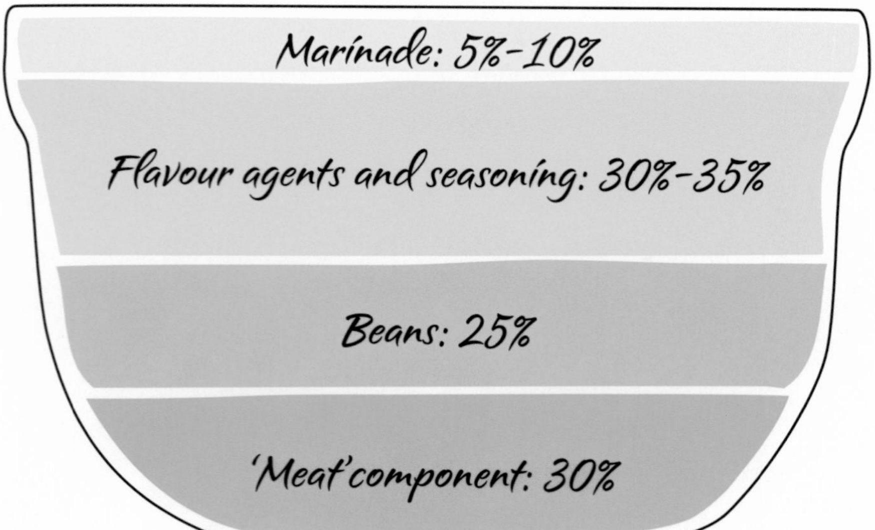

Marinade: 5%-10%

Flavour agents and seasoning: 30%-35%

Beans: 25%

'Meat' component: 30%

RECIPE:	VITAL 'V' BURGER	VEGAN QUARTER POUNDER
BEANS	200g tinned chickpeas or beans	200g tinned black beans
FLAVOUR AGENTS AND SEASONING	100g tomato purée 100ml veg stock 4 tbsp nutritional yeast 2 tbsp tamari or soy sauce 1 tbsp Dijon mustard 1 tsp garlic powder 1 tsp smoked paprika ½ tsp freshly ground black pepper Pinch of salt	100ml veg stock 2 tbsp tamari or soy sauce 2 tbsp pesto of choice (see p. 165) 2 tsp paprika 1 tsp garlic powder 1 tsp onion powder ½ tsp freshly ground black pepper Pinch of salt
'MEAT' COMPONENT	250g vital wheat gluten	250g vital wheat gluten
MARINADE	6 tbsp tamari or soy sauce 1 tbsp maple syrup 1 tsp smoked paprika	4 tbsp tamari or soy sauce 1 tsp maple syrup 1 tsp paprika
OIL	1 tbsp oil	1 tbsp oil

Makes 6 burgers

1. Drain and rinse the beans, then mash them in a bowl with a potato masher or pulse in a food processor. Add all the flavour agents and seasoning and mix well.

2. Transfer this mix to a large bowl and add the 'meat' component. Mix until thoroughly combined and the mixture comes together into a tight dough ball. Tip out on to a clean work surface and knead the dough with your hands for 5 to 10 minutes, to encourage the gluten to become tougher and give the burgers more elasticity.

3. Divide the dough into 6 equal portions (aim for about 150g for each burger), then shape into patties, flattening them to even out the shape.

4. Set up a steamer over a pot of water and bring the water to a boil. Wrap each burger in foil, making sure that each one is completely enclosed. Place all the wrapped burgers in the steamer, cover and steam for about 20 minutes. Carefully remove from the heat and allow to cool slightly before unwrapping. The steamed burgers can be stored in a sealed container in the fridge for up to 3 days at this stage.

5. Mix all the marinade ingredients together in a bowl. Dip the burgers in the marinade, coating them well.

6. Heat the oil in a large non-stick frying pan on a high heat. Add the burgers to the hot pan and cook on each side until nicely browned and starting to char. Cook the burgers in batches or in two pans if necessary so that you don't crowd the pan.

7. Assemble the cooked burgers with whatever buns, sauces and toppings you like – and don't forget the fries on p. 139!

TVP BURGERS

Textured vegetable protein (TVP) is also known as soy protein, which is a more accurate name as it is made exclusively from soy rather than actual veg. TVP is a dehydrated product, usually bought as granules, that has a texture that resembles minced beef once it's cooked. It cooks quickly and has a protein content as high as 70%, but it's also a highly processed ingredient, so it's best to consume it in moderation.

Making burgers with TVP requires one part liquid to one part TVP (in terms of volume). Like vital wheat gluten, TVP is bland on its own, so it needs to be mixed with plenty of flavour agents. We normally add garlic and onion powder, spices and tamari or soy sauce, and we tend to use vegetable stock or tomato purée instead of simply using water. We also add some tinned beans and pan-fried mushrooms (or something similar) to give it more bite and more nutrition. Then it's simply a matter of shaping your mix into burgers and frying them in a little oil in a hot pan.

Flavour agents and seasoning: 15%
Binder: 5%
Beans: 25%
Added veg: 20%
Liquid: 25%
TVP: 10%

Makes 5 to 6 burgers

1. Put the TVP and all the flavour agents and seasoning into a medium-sized bowl and stir to combine, then pour over the liquid, making sure the warm veg stock or water covers the TVP. Set aside for 10 minutes to rehydrate the TVP. It should fluff up and turn firm. (The ground flax seeds aren't really a flavour agent per se, but they're added at this stage to help bind the TVP together and to enhance the protein and structure of the burger.)

2. Drain and rinse the beans, then tip them into a bowl and mash with a potato masher. Set aside.

3. To prepare the added veg, peel and finely chop the onions (if using) and garlic. Chop the mushrooms (if using). Heat the oil in a large frying pan on a medium-high heat. Add the onions (if using), garlic and mushrooms (if using) and cook for 4 to 6 minutes, until starting to turn golden. For the mushroom burger add the tamari or soy sauce and cook for 1 minute, stirring all the time. Add the mashed beans to the pan.

4. Drain the TVP and squeeze it to remove any excess water, then add to the pan with the extra flavour agents and cook for 2 minutes.

5. Remove the pan from the heat and allow to cool before adding the binder ingredients. Stir well, until the mixture holds its shape. Shape into 130g to 150g patties. You can store the uncooked burgers in an airtight container in the fridge for up to 3 days at this stage.

6. Heat another splash of oil in a large non-stick frying pan on a medium heat. Add the burgers to the hot pan and fry for 2 to 3 minutes on each side, until nicely charred and cooked through. (Cook the burgers in batches or in two pans if necessary so that you don't crowd the pan.) Alternatively, you could bake the burgers in the oven. Rub each side of the burgers lightly with a little oil and place on a baking tray. Bake in the oven at 180°C fan/400°F/gas 6 for 20 minutes, flipping them over halfway through.

7. Assemble the cooked burgers with whatever buns, sauces and toppings you like – and don't forget the fries on p. 139!

RECIPE:	MEATY MUSHROOM BURGER	MEATY VEG BURGER
TVP	100g TVP	100g TVP
FLAVOUR AGENTS AND SEASONING	½ a small raw beetroot, peeled and grated 2 tbsp ground flax seeds 1 tbsp tamari or soy sauce 1 tsp salt ½ tsp freshly ground black pepper	100g tomato purée 2 tbsp ground flax seeds 2 tbsp nut butter (blend with a splash of warm water first to loosen) 1 tbsp tamari or soy sauce 1 tsp paprika ½ tsp freshly ground black pepper
LIQUID	300ml warm veg stock or water, to cover	300ml warm veg stock or water, to cover
BEANS	1 × 400g tin of chickpeas	1 × 400g tin of kidney beans
ADDED VEG	200g oyster or chestnut mushrooms 1 garlic clove 1 tbsp oil	2 medium onions 2 garlic cloves 1 tbsp oil
EXTRA FLAVOUR AGENTS	1 tbsp tamari or soy sauce ½ tsp onion powder ½ tsp garlic powder	2 tbsp tamari or soy sauce 2 tbsp nutritional yeast 1 tsp paprika
BINDER	4 tbsp rice flour 4 tbsp psyllium husks	4 tbsp rice flour 4 tbsp psyllium husks

← BREAKDOWN →

DO YOU WANT FRIES WITH THAT?

We love a side of chips or French fries to accompany our burger. Even when we're feeling particularly pious and health conscious, the smell of hot fries fresh out of the oven calls our name like nothing else! Here are our top tips for making fries and wedges.

Leave the skin on the spuds, as the skin is where most of the fibre is. We know you're not eating chips for their health-giving properties, but you may as well make them a little healthier if you can.

Bake your chips or fries in the oven rather than cooking them in a deep-fat fryer. If you're seeking the ultimate low-fat fries, then consider buying an air fryer – these are widely available now. It functions just like a deep-fat fryer except that instead of oil, hot air is used to crisp up your fries. They won't be quite as satiating as fries cooked with oil, but they will be crispy and crunchy, starchy and sweet.

Sweet potato fries are becoming more and more popular these days, because they are higher in nutrition than regular potatoes and just as delicious. They can be cooked in the same way, but they will never crisp up to the same degree as a regular potato.

RECIPE:	MATCHSTICKS	WEDGES	SWEET POTATO MATCHSTICKS	SWEET POTATO WEDGES
SPUDS	1kg potatoes	1kg potatoes	1kg sweet potatoes	1kg sweet potatoes
CUT	Matchsticks	Chunky cut	Matchsticks	Chunky cut
OIL	2 tbsp	4 tbsp	2 tbsp	4 tbsp
SALT	1 tsp	1 tsp	1 tsp	1 tsp

BREAKDOWN ↑ ↓

Serves 4

1. To make matchstick fries using either regular or sweet potatoes, preheat the oven to 180°C fan/400°F/gas 6. Toss to coat the spuds in the oil and salt, then spread the fries out on one or two baking trays, making sure the tray(s) aren't too crowded so that plenty of air can circulate around the fries. Bake in the preheated oven for 30 minutes – that's it! No rotation and no parboiling required.

2. To make potato and sweet potato wedges, preheat the oven to 200°C fan/425°F/gas 7. Toss to coat the spuds in the oil and salt, then spread the wedges out on one or two baking trays, making sure the tray(s) aren't too crowded so that plenty of air can circulate around the wedges. Bake in the preheated oven for 40 minutes, shaking and rotating the trays halfway through the cooking time.

Pizza

When we started making pizza in the café about a decade ago, Steve would make about 20 litres of dough at a time and leave it to ferment overnight in the fridge, then shape it on big cast-iron trays to make deep-crust pizza that was jam-packed with veg and a rich tomato sauce that would always get rave reviews. Steve got a wood-fired pizza oven for Christmas last year, so we've been spending a lot of time at the weekends perfecting our dough and coming up with the perfect vegan pizza.

THE ESSENTIALS

A pizza is made up of the following four essential elements:

- **Dough:** This is usually a base of white flour, which makes up the starch element.

- **Tomato sauce:** The sauce adds colour, sweetness, moisture and acidity.

- **Cheese:** Cheese adds fat, salt and moisture.

- **Toppings:** Your favourite toppings add colour, texture and flavour.

PIZZA DOUGH

Makes enough for 6 to 10 pizzas

Our basic dough is based on the classic Neapolitan pizza, which uses only four ingredients: flour, water, salt and yeast. A typical 30cm pizza, if stretched out thin, will require 150g to 200g of risen dough.

The secret to a dough with a strong flavour and good elasticity is letting it ferment in the fridge for 1 to 5 days. During fermentation, the starch in the flour will break down to simple sugars, the yeast will create flavourful by-products and the gluten will develop and relax, allowing you to stretch the dough without it ripping or bouncing back. However, we realize that most people aren't searching for the perfect dough and might prefer a quicker option that will be ready in 2 hours, so simply knead the dough more at the start and increase the temperature when the dough proves. If there are any Italians reading this, please skip ahead to the next paragraph now – we have also included a recipe for a dough that you can make instantly using baking powder instead of yeast.

Dough freezes well for up to 6 months. Just make a batch and portion it out into 150g to 200g balls, then wrap each one really well in cling film and put it straight into the freezer. To cook, simply unwrap your dough balls, place each one on a separate plate, cover again with cling film and let them thaw in the fridge overnight.

A NOTE ON FLOUR

The flour that is most commonly used for pizza is '00' flour, which is a soft white flour that has a protein content of around 10%. We are all about using whole grains and using brown flour over white, but when it comes to pizza, if you try to make it too 'healthy' or make a 100% wholemeal dough, it will taste more like toasted bread with toppings rather than the classic pizza you're probably craving. If your goal is flavour, you want to go with a 100% strong white flour or '00' flour. If you're aiming for a middle ground, use 50% strong white flour and 50% wholemeal flour.

Gluten-free dough

If you want to try a gluten-free dough, you have many options. For a more conventional option, use a gluten-free white flour. For a healthier option, use buckwheat flour. Just be aware that since both flours are gluten free, you won't be able to develop any elasticity in the dough and it will lack the chew of a traditional dough once it's baked.

Using 1kg gluten-free flour to 500ml water (a 50% hydration) and 4 teaspoons (20g) of salt, simply mix to combine into a dough, then roll it out as thin as you like. Bake the dough first in an oven preheated to its highest temperature for 8 to 10 minutes, until it seals, a little like blind baking a shortcrust pastry, then add your sauce, vegan cheese and toppings and bake it again until the cheese has melted and the sauce and toppings are warmed through.

RECIPE:	NO YEAST QUICK DOUGH	BASIC DOUGH	FERMENTED DOUGH
WATER	600ml water	650ml warm water (37°C)	700ml warm water (37°C)
BAKING POWDER OR YEAST	1½ tbsp baking powder	2 × 7g sachets of fast action dried yeast or 14g dried active yeast	2 × 7g sachets of fast action dried yeast or 14g dried active yeast
OIL			2 tbsp olive oil
FLOUR	1kg '00' or strong white flour	1kg '00' or strong white flour	1kg '00' or strong white flour
SALT	4 tsp salt (20g)	4 tsp salt (20g)	4 tsp salt (20g)

← BREAKDOWN →

1. To make the no yeast quick dough, simply put the water, baking powder, flour and salt into a large bowl and mix to combine, then tip out on to a lightly floured work surface and knead for 5 to 8 minutes, until the dough feels nice and soft. Divide into 150g to 200g balls, then roll out each one to fit the size of your pizza pan.

2. Cook using the blind bake tray method (see p. 160) before adding your sauce, toppings and cheese.

3. To make the basic dough or fermented dough, first ensure your water is around 37°C (body temperature), as this will help the yeast to activate quickly. A simple way to achieve this is to add one third or 33% of the total volume of water required of just-boiled water to two-thirds or 66% of the total volume of water required of cold water. Put the warm water into a large bowl (or the bowl of your stand mixer if you don't want to knead by hand), then add the yeast and oil (if using).

4. To knead your dough by hand, add the flour and salt to the water, then mix until it comes together into a rough dough. Tip the dough out on to a lightly floured work surface. If the dough is really sticky at this stage, add a little dusting of flour. Start kneading by using the heel of your hand to press and roll the dough across the worktop, then use your other hand to return it to the start while at the same time folding it over. Avoid adding any more flour – it will lose its stickiness as you work and come together beautifully.

5. Continue kneading for about 10 minutes, until the gluten has developed enough for the dough to pass the windowpane test – if you hold your dough up to the light and stretch it, you should be able to see light through the dough, like a windowpane, without it ripping.

6. Alternatively, you can use a stand mixer using the dough hook attachment. As above, add the flour and salt to the water (which already has the yeast and oil, if using, added), then mix on a medium speed for 6 to 8 minutes, until it passes the windowpane test.

7. Once your dough passes the windowpane test, it's time to shape the dough. Divide the dough into 150g to 200g balls (1kg of flour should give you around 10 × 165g balls). Place each ball into a large container and dust with a little flour to make it easier to handle. Cover tightly with a lid or cling film.

8. If you're making the basic dough, leave it out at room temperature for 2 to 5 hours. The higher the room temperature, the quicker it will rise. A simple indicator that your dough is ready is that it has doubled in volume. If you're making the fermented dough, put it into the fridge for anywhere from 1 to 5 days.

9. Take the dough out of the fridge 2 hours before you want to cook your pizzas to make it easier to roll the dough, then roll out each base as thick or thin as you would like, ready for the sauce, cheese and toppings to be added.

10. The easiest way to roll your dough is to use a rolling pin until it's nice and thin (just make sure your rolling pin and work surface are well dusted with flour). If you prefer to do it by hand, flatten your dough, then, starting in the centre, push the air out to the edges, again ensuring that your hands are well dusted in flour to prevent them sticking. Repeat until the dough is nice and flat. If it's bouncing back and is too elastic, take a little break for 5 minutes to allow the gluten to relax – when you come back, it will be a lot easier to shape. Shape the pizza 25cm to 30cm in diameter.

PIZZA SAUCES

Makes 500ml

You could always use a good-quality shop-bought tomato sauce, but it's so easy to make your own and the flavour is always so much better. We've given you a framework for three simple sauces, but to add a little extra flavour, try using a garlic- or chilli-infused olive oil instead of regular olive oil.

Our favourite way to bump up the flavour in a tomato sauce and to make it more full-bodied is to simply add some pesto to it. We use two parts tomato sauce to one part pesto, so start with 1 × 400g tin of chopped tomatoes and add approx. 200g of your pesto of choice. We've used different pestos in the recipe framework overleaf, but you could use any of the pesto sauces on pp. 165–7.

1. To make the basic tomato sauce, first peel and finely chop the garlic. Heat the olive oil in a saucepan on a medium heat. Add the garlic and fry for 1 minute, until fragrant, taking care that it doesn't burn or else it will make your sauce bitter. Add the tinned tomatoes and bring to the boil, then reduce the heat and simmer for 5 minutes.

2. Taste and adjust the seasoning with a little sweetener to counteract the acidity of the tinned tomatoes and some salt and pepper.

3. To make the roasted red pepper pesto sauce or tomato and basil pesto sauce, simply mix the olive oil, tomatoes and pesto in a bowl until combined. Taste and adjust the seasoning with salt and pepper and you're ready to go!

RECIPE:	BASIC TOMATO SAUCE	ROASTED RED PEPPER PESTO SAUCE	TOMATO AND BASIL PESTO SAUCE
GARLIC	2 garlic cloves		
OLIVE OIL	3 tbsp olive oil	1 tbsp olive oil	1 tbsp olive oil
TOMATOES	1 × 400g tin of chopped tomatoes	1 × 400g tin of chopped tomatoes	1 × 400g tin of chopped tomatoes
PESTO		200g roasted red pepper pesto (p. 167)	200g basil pesto (p. 167)
SWEETENER	½ tbsp maple syrup		
SEASONING	Salt and freshly ground black pepper	Salt and freshly ground black pepper	Salt and freshly ground black pepper

BREAKDOWN ↑↓

FOOLPROOF VEGAN MOZZARELLA

Makes approx. 18 x 30g balls (the picture on page 154 shows a double batch)

In our humble opinion, store-bought vegan cheese hasn't been able to adequately mimic dairy cheese yet. Often it's simply a fat, such as coconut oil, mixed with a starch and binder, and a natural flavour is added to make it taste like the cheese it's trying to re-create. When making pizza at home, we use this vegan mozzarella that easily fools the non-vegans!

100g cashews

200ml water

4 tablespoons olive oil

3 tablespoons tapioca flour, arrowroot flour or rice flour

1 tablespoon nutritional yeast

1½ teaspoons apple cider vinegar

1 teaspoon salt

¼ teaspoon garlic powder

For the brine:

400ml water

¾ tablespoon salt

1. Fill and boil the kettle. Put the cashews into a medium-sized saucepan and cover with boiling water. Bring to the boil on a high heat, then reduce to a simmer and cook for 5 to 10 minutes.

2. Drain and rinse the cashews, then put them in a blender along with the 200ml of fresh water and the rest of the ingredients and blend until smooth. The smoother your mixture, the smoother your cheese will be, so try to ensure there are no lumps or visible pieces of cashew.

3. To make the brine, put the 400ml of water and the salt into a large bowl or jar and stir until the salt has dissolved.

4. Pour the cashew mixture into a non-stick frying pan or saucepan and stir constantly on a high heat for 5 to 10 minutes, until it starts to thicken and bubble. The mixture will eventually come together into a ball and will start to leave the bottom of the pan. When it does, remove the pan from the heat.

5. Once the mixture is cool enough to handle, with wet fingers to prevent sticking, pinch off bits and roll them into small balls about the size of a ping pong ball, or else use two tablespoons to shape it into small balls.

6. Simply pop each ball into the brine. The mozzarella will keep like this, covered, in the fridge for up to 1 week.

TOPPINGS

Makes 1 x 30cm pizza

We like to have lots of variety when it comes to our pizza toppings. You can't beat the simplicity of a classic Margherita, but if we're going for the all singing, all dancing supreme pizza, we'll add a thin layer of everything.

From all the pizzas we've made in Steve's wood-fired oven, we've learned that the keys to making pizza at home are preparation and organization. So as a first step, prep your veg and roast them in the oven. While the veg are roasting, make your tomato sauce, pesto and vegan mozzarella (or use shop-bought versions). Have all the components ready to go and laid out on the counter in separate bowls.

- **Vegetables:** You will need to cook all your veg toppings before you add them to the pizza. Even when we make pizza in Steve's wood-fired pizza oven at 500°C, the veg won't cook fully if we don't pre-cook them first. Chop all your veg into bite-size pieces, then put them all into a bowl, drizzle with a little oil and season with a generous pinch of salt, tossing to coat. Spread them out evenly on a baking tray so they have room to brown on all sides, and roast in the oven at 200°C fan/425°F/gas 7 for about 20 minutes.

- **Barbecued oyster mushrooms or jackfruit:** One of our favourite toppings is barbecued pulled oyster mushrooms or jackfruit. It's a flavour bomb of a pizza with a nice 'grizzly' texture too. Simply rip up some oyster mushrooms or some drained and rinsed tinned jackfruit lengthways, then coat with the BBQ ketchup on p. 323. You want to half-cook them before they go on the pizza so that they are completely cooked through by the time the pizza comes out of the oven, so put them on a baking tray and bake in the oven for 15 minutes at 200°C fan/425°F/gas 7, until they start to crisp around the edges.

- **Vegan sausages:** We cook our homemade vegan sausages (see p. 64) beforehand, then slice them up to go on the pizzas – or you can use your favourite store-bought vegan sausages.

- **Pesto:** A drizzle of your favourite pesto will add lots more flavour.

- **Greens or herbs:** We always like to have some greens or fresh herbs, such as rocket, baby spinach or fresh basil leaves, on top of our pizzas to add freshness and vibrancy.

- **Pickles or chillies:** Quick pickles such as pickled red onions or Asian-style pickled carrot strips (see p. 308) add a pop of colour and acid to your pizza when strewn on top after it comes out of the oven.

- **Nuts:** Sprinkle some pine nuts on top just before serving to add more texture and bite.

1. Preheat your oven to its highest temperature. Have all the ingredients ready to go and laid out on the counter in separate bowls.

2. See page 160 for how to prepare the dough and cook the pizza with the sauce, cheese and toppings. You'll probably get only one or two pizzas in your oven at a time, so if we're feeding a good few people, we'll keep making pizzas and serving them for sharing as soon as they come out of the oven.

3. When the pizza comes out of the oven, drizzle over a little pesto (if using), add a small handful of greens or fresh herbs, then add your garnish.

→

RECIPE:	CLASSIC MARGHERITA	ALL SINGING, ALL DANCING	SAUSAGE, BASIL PESTO AND MOZZARELLA	GREEN PIZZA	MUSHROOM, PINEAPPLE AND SUN-DRIED TOMATO PESTO
DOUGH	150g to 200g risen pizza dough ball (p. 145)	150g to 200g risen pizza dough ball (p. 145)	150g to 200g risen pizza dough ball (p. 145)	150g to 200g risen pizza dough ball (p. 145)	150g to 200g risen pizza dough ball (p. 145)
SAUCE	Basic tomato sauce (p. 152)	Roasted red pepper pesto sauce (p. 152)	Tomato and basil pesto sauce (p. 152)	Basil pesto (p. 167)	Roasted red pepper pesto sauce (p. 152)
CHEESE	Vegan mozzarella (p. 155)	Vegan mozzarella (p. 155)	Vegan mozzarella (p. 155)	Vegan mozzarella (p. 155)	Vegan Cheddar or feta
TOPPINGS		Roasted mixed veg (aubergines, courgettes and mixed peppers – see pp. 298–300) BBQ oyster mushrooms or shredded jackfruit (see p. 157) Artichoke hearts	Cooked and sliced vegan sausages (p. 64) Roasted mixed veg (aubergines, courgettes and mixed peppers – see pp. 298–300)	Roasted courgettes (p. 298) Asparagus Green olives	Thinly sliced pan-fried mushrooms (p. 300) Pineapple chunks
PESTO		Pesto of choice (p. 167)	Basil pesto (p. 167)	Basil pesto (p. 167)	Pesto of choice (p. 167)
GREENS AND FRESH HERBS	Fresh basil leaves	Small handful of rocket	Fresh basil leaves	Small handful of baby spinach	Small handful of rocket
GARNISH	Chilli oil	Chilli oil or chilli flakes Pine nuts	Pickled red onions (p. 308) Artichoke hearts	Chilli flakes	Pine nuts

BREAKDOWN ↑ ↓

HOW TO COOK PIZZA AT HOME

It's almost impossible to re-create the pizza you get from a wood-fired oven, which reaches temperatures of 400°C to 500°C, but you can still do an excellent job at home with a regular oven. Here are our two favourite ways of cooking pizzas in a home oven.

The blind bake tray method

This method gives great results. Preheat your oven as hot as it will go. Get a large baking tray and cover it with non-stick baking paper. Lightly flour your work surface.

Using a rolling pin, roll out your dough ball thinly (it should be approx. 150g to 200g) until it fits the shape of the baking tray. Carefully transfer the dough to the baking tray. Using a fork, gently pierce the dough all over so that it doesn't bubble up as it bakes.

Bake the pizza dough in the preheated oven for 8 to 10 minutes, until it starts to dry out and is turning light brown. Remove from the oven and add a light layer of sauce, spreading it right to the edges. Add a light dusting of cheese and toppings, then return to the oven and bake for 6 to 10 minutes more, until the cheese has melted, the toppings are heated through and the crust is golden brown. Slide the pizza off the tray on to a cutting board, then cut into slices.

The pizza stone or oven tile method

This method will give your dough a lovely crisp crust. Preheat your oven to its highest temperature and put your pizza stone or oven tile inside the oven as it preheats. (A pizza stone is used in the photograph on p. 150.)

Lightly flour your work surface and roll out a pizza dough ball (which should be approx. 150g to 200g), using a rolling pin or stretching it by hand. If you want a big crust and have used a rolling pin, simply roll back the edges of your dough to form a crust. Alternatively, use your fingers instead of the rolling pin and gently press the air from the risen dough ball out to the edges of the dough until your pizza base is approx. 30cm.

Before removing your pizza stone from the oven, decide where you are going to safely land it and have some sturdy oven gloves ready. Being very careful and using the oven gloves, remove your hot pizza stone from the oven. Remove the oven gloves, then add a light dusting of flour to the pizza stone and carefully place your dough on top. Add a light layer of sauce, spreading it right to the edges. Add a light dusting of cheese and toppings, being careful not to touch the hot stone. Put the oven gloves back on, then put the assembled pizza back into the oven.

Bake in the preheated oven for 10 to 15 minutes, until the cheese has melted, the toppings are heated through and the crust is golden brown. Remove from the oven and transfer to a cutting board, then cut into slices.

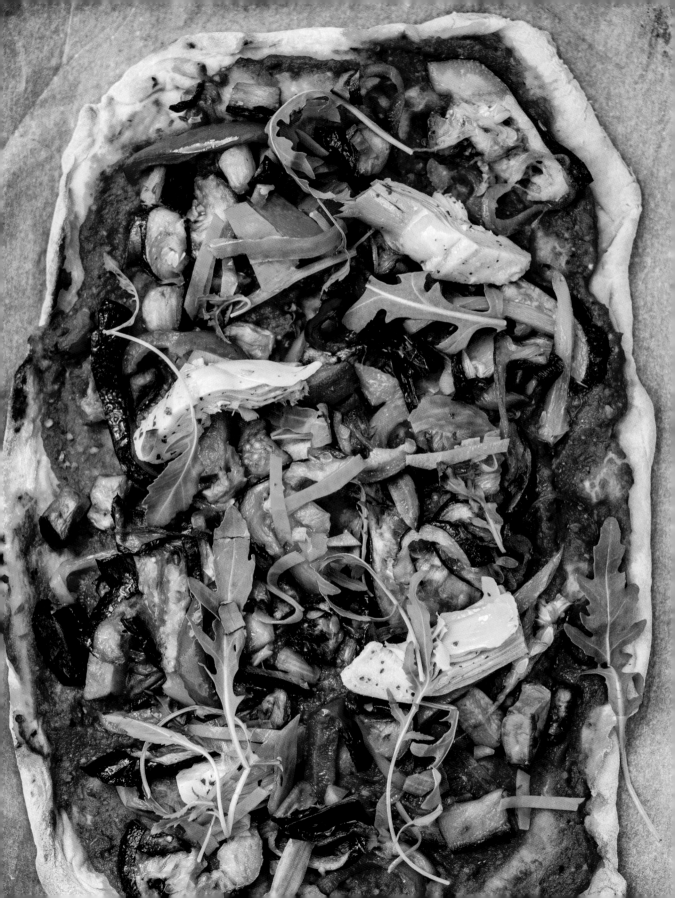

Pasta

We didn't have pasta until we were about 10 years old. It was a novelty in Ireland back then, but now it's ubiquitous and is an everyday food that forms the basis of so many simple, easy meals that you can make in minutes.

There are around 310 different types of pasta, in all shapes and sizes. These days you can also find pasta that's made with more unusual ingredients other than the traditional durum wheat, such as black beans, rice flour, red lentils and other legumes, to make it gluten free and higher in protein. Our preference is to use wholemeal pasta or brown pasta where possible, as it's higher in fibre and nutrition than regular white pasta. Wholemeal or brown pasta won't taste as indulgent as white, but when served with a good sauce, most people won't notice.

We have divided this chapter into two sections: sauces and baked pasta dishes. The sauces section is broken down into seven different types, each of which can be paired with your favourite type of pasta for a quick dinner. As a rule of thumb allow 100g of dried pasta per person, so a 500g packet of pasta should serve five people.

In the second section we have included three types of baked pasta dishes: lasagne, cannelloni and pasta bakes. In baked pasta dishes the heat cooks from all sides, which intensifies the flavour and also develops a nice crisp crust on top.

PESTO

We make a vast amount of pesto every week to sell in our own shop and cafés as well as supermarkets nationwide. We make three types of pesto – our Lovely Basil Pesto, Sun-dried Tomato Pesto and Gorgeous Cashew Pesto – which are all based on the same framework.

THE ESSENTIALS

Fresh herbs or greens: As a general rule, use 50g of your fresh herb of choice, such as basil, coriander, parsley, mint or wild garlic (start with a little less wild garlic, 40g, since it's so strong). When using leafy greens, such as spinach, kale or collard greens, as opposed to herbs, start with 50g and increase it up to 75g if needed for the flavour to carry through. When making pesto we don't use the stalks of any herbs or greens, as these often don't blend very well and generally don't have the same flavour as the leaf.

Toasted nuts: Use 100g of toasted cashews, pine nuts or your choice of nut. For example, walnuts work well in a wild garlic pesto and small almond chunks give our sun-dried tomato pesto a meaty texture, while cashews give a pesto a creamy mouthfeel. It's always best to toast your nuts, as they will develop more flavour through browning and lose some moisture, which further intensifies the flavour. See p. 301 for instructions on how to toast nuts.

Garlic: Use 3 medium cloves of garlic per batch.

Oil: Use 150ml of a light-tasting olive oil or an oil of your choice. (To make a low-fat pesto, use 75ml of water and 75ml of oil, but the trade-off is that this will shorten the pesto's shelf life, as it's now higher in water.) We like to use a neutral-tasting oil rather than a strong-tasting olive oil, as the main flavour of the pesto should be the garlic and herb of choice, balanced with the nuts and salt – the oil is merely the carrier of those flavours.

Acid: Use 2 to 3 teaspoons of acid, such as lemon or lime juice, apple cider vinegar or balsamic vinegar, etc.

Salt: In general start with 1 teaspoon of salt, then taste after blending the pesto and add a little more if the pesto tastes flat.

1. Strip the leaves from your fresh herbs or greens and discard the stalks. Peel and roughly chop the garlic (if using). If using greens, simply blanch them in boiling water for 2 minutes, then cool them under cold water for a minute or two. Drain them and squeeze out any extra moisture.

2. Put the herbs or cooked greens, garlic, toasted nuts, extra ingredients (if using), oil, acid and salt into a food processor or blender and blend to your desired consistency. If you blend for longer it will be smoother and more homogeneous, whereas if you pulse it your pesto will be chunky. Taste and adjust the seasoning with a little more salt or acid if the pesto tastes flat.

3. To serve, simply stir the pesto through your hot cooked pasta. Use any of the pestos opposite with 300g to 350g of dried pasta or a 2:1 ratio of pasta to pesto (spaghetti, tagliatelle and fusilli all work fab). We like a lot of pesto with our pasta, but if you prefer less, just use more pasta or less pesto.

4. If you would like your pesto to be a little more saucy, add a little reserved pasta cooking water to loosen it until it reaches your desired consistency. We also love to serve pesto with penne as a cold pasta salad with rocket and halved cherry tomatoes.

RECIPE:	WILD GARLIC PESTO	KALE PESTO	CORIANDER PESTO	BASIL PESTO	ROASTED RED PEPPER PESTO
FRESH HERBS OR GREENS	40g wild garlic	50g steamed kale (p. 300)	50g fresh coriander	50g fresh basil	30g fresh basil
GARLIC		3 garlic cloves	3 garlic cloves	3 garlic cloves	3 garlic cloves
TOASTED NUTS	100g toasted walnuts (p. 301)	100g toasted cashews (p. 301)	100g toasted cashews (p. 301)	100g toasted pine nuts (p. 301)	100g almonds (p. 301)
EXTRA INGREDIENTS					100g roasted red peppers from a jar, drained
OIL	150ml olive oil	150ml sunflower oil	150ml olive oil	150ml olive oil	150ml olive oil
ACID	2 tsp apple cider vinegar	Juice of 1 lime	Juice of 1 lime	2 tsp lemon juice	1 tbsp balsamic vinegar 2 tsp lemon juice
SALT	1 tsp salt	1 tsp salt	1 tsp salt	¾ tsp salt	1 tsp salt

BREAKDOWN ↑ ↓

OIL-BASED SAUCES

Serves 3 to 4

Spaghetti aglio e olio ('garlic and oil'), also known as poor man's pasta, is a classic Italian dish and also one of the simplest. However, because the sauce is just oil mixed with pasta cooking water, it can be quite high in calories (oil contains around 120 calories per tablespoon). But for those times when the cupboards are bare, these are handy recipes to have in your repertoire.

1. Cook the pasta in a large pot of boiling salted water according to the packet instructions, until al dente (and see p. 197), making sure you reserve a mugful of the pasta cooking water before you drain it. This is very important, as this starchy cooking water will help to emulsify the oil into a sauce – without it, your dish will just taste greasy.

2. Peel and finely chop the garlic. To prepare the extras, deseed and finely chop the chilli (if using). Finely chop the radicchio and chop the drained artichoke hearts (if using). To prepare the fresh herbs, finely chop the parsley or sage leaves or tear the basil leaves.

3. Put your largest frying pan on a high heat – the pan needs to be big enough to also accommodate all the cooked pasta at the end. Once the pan is hot, reduce the heat to medium and add the olive oil, then add the garlic and cook for about 1 minute, stirring constantly, until golden but not browned. If you burn the garlic at this stage it will make the entire dish taste bitter, so it's best to throw it out and start again if that happens.

4. Add the cooked pasta to the pan along with the salt and 1 tablespoon of the reserved cooking water to start with. Stir well to emulsify the oil and the pasta water. Add more of the reserved cooking water 1 tablespoon at a time, mixing well each time, until a nice creamy sauce is formed. Always start by adding just a little pasta cooking water at a time, because if you add too much you will have to cook your pasta and sauce for longer to thicken the sauce, which means your pasta will overcook.

5. Stir in the extras and fresh herbs (if using). If the pasta and sauce seem too dry, add a little more pasta water to loosen. Taste and adjust the seasoning with a little more salt if needed, then serve straight away.

→

RECIPE:	AGLIO E OLIO	CHILLI AND BASIL	LEMON AND SAGE	ARTICHOKE AND RADICCHIO
DRIED PASTA	150g spaghetti	150g tagliatelle	150g fusilli	150g linguine
OLIVE OIL	5 tbsp olive oil	5 tbsp olive oil	6 tbsp olive oil	5 tbsp olive oil
GARLIC	4 garlic cloves	4 garlic cloves	4 garlic cloves	4 garlic cloves
SALT	¾ tsp salt	¾ tsp salt	¾ tsp salt	¾ tsp salt
EXTRAS		1 fresh red chilli	Juice of ½ a lemon Zest of ½ a lemon 4 tbsp grated vegan Parmesan	200g artichoke hearts from a jar Zest of ½ a lemon
FRESH HERBS	20g fresh flat-leaf parsley	15g fresh basil leaves	10g fresh sage leaves	½ a head of radicchio, chopped

BREAKDOWN ↑↓

TOMATO-BASED SAUCES

Makes 1 litre

There are infinite variations of tomato sauces depending on what you add, how you cook it or where you are in the world, as it will have a different name depending on what country or region you're in. We've given you a basic tomato sauce recipe and two variations (the sweet potato and mushroom tomato sauce is a thick sauce that works really well with lasagne), but play around with other additions to boost the flavour, such as capers, olives, sun-dried tomatoes, artichoke hearts and fresh herbs.

Each recipe in the framework makes about 1 litre, which is enough to serve with 500g of dried pasta.

1. Peel and finely chop the garlic. Deseed the chilli (if using) if you don't want the extra heat, then finely chop. Include the seeds if you like it spicier.

2. Heat the olive oil in a medium-sized saucepan on a medium heat. Add the prepared base veg and cook for 3 to 4 minutes, then add the garlic and chilli (if using) and cook for 1 to 2 minutes, until softened and starting to brown. Add the veg or protein (if using) and cook for 3 to 4 minutes more, until softened.

3. Add the tomatoes, wine (if using), lentils and other extras (if using), sweetener and salt. Bring to the boil, then reduce to a simmer. The longer you leave the sauce to simmer, the more intense and concentrated it will become as the water evaporates and the flavours intensify. We normally leave it to reduce for 10 minutes, stirring occasionally.

4. Taste and adjust the seasoning with a little more sweetener, acid or salt if needed. Trust your palate here and only add more salt if the sauce tastes flat. If it tastes heavy, add some acid to cut through it. If it tastes too sharp, balance it out with a little more sweetener.

5. To serve, simply stir the sauce through your hot cooked pasta, then garnish with torn fresh basil leaves (if using) and don't forget some grated vegan Parmesan for sprinkling over.

BREAKDOWN RECIPE:	TOMATO SAUCE WITH LENTILS	SIMPLE SPICY CHILLI AND GARLIC TOMATO SAUCE	SWEET POTATO AND MUSHROOM TOMATO SAUCE
GARLIC AND CHILLI	2 garlic cloves	3 garlic cloves 1 fresh red chilli	3 garlic cloves 1 fresh red chilli
OLIVE OIL	2 tbsp olive oil	3 tbsp olive oil	2 tbsp olive oil
BASE VEG	1 onion, finely diced 1 small carrot, grated 2 stalks of celery, diced		200g mushrooms of choice
VEG OR PROTEIN	1 × 400g tin lentils, drained and rinsed		400g roasted sweet potato (p. 300)
TOMATOES	1 × 680ml jar of passata	2 × 400g tins of chopped tomatoes	2 × 400g tins of chopped tomatoes 100g tomato purée 5 sun-dried tomatoes (not the kind in oil), finely chopped
WINE	100ml red wine		100ml red wine
HERBS	1 bay leaf	1 bay leaf	1 bay leaf A few sprigs of fresh thyme
SWEETENER	1 tbsp maple syrup	1 tbsp maple syrup	1½ tbsp maple syrup
SALT	1½ tsp salt	1½ tsp salt	1 tsp salt
GARNISH	Fresh basil leaves, torn Grated vegan Parmesan	Fresh basil leaves, torn Grated vegan Parmesan	Grated vegan Parmesan

BÉCHAMEL SAUCES

Makes 500ml

A béchamel (or white sauce) is a milk-based sauce that is thickened with a roux. A roux is the French name for a combination of equal parts fat and starch that is cooked until it starts to brown and is used to thicken sauces, soups or stews. A traditional roux uses butter, but our vegan version uses olive oil and a non-dairy milk (usually unsweetened oat, soya or almond milk, but you can use whichever milk you prefer). The béchamel is then seasoned with a bay leaf, nutmeg, salt, pepper and any other spices that take your fancy.

We recommend serving either of these two white sauces with 200g of dried pasta to serve two people.

1. Pour the non-dairy milk into a small saucepan, then add the flavour agents and seasoning and the herbs. Bring to the boil, then reduce the heat and simmer for a few minutes to allow the flavours to infuse. The longer you let it simmer, the stronger the flavours will be.

2. Meanwhile, to make the roux, heat the olive oil in a medium-sized saucepan on a medium heat. Once the oil is hot, sift in the flour and cook for 1 to 2 minutes, stirring constantly with a whisk, until golden.

3. Remove the onion half from the infused milk, then slowly pour the milk into the pan with the roux, stirring constantly. Bring to the boil, then reduce the heat to a simmer, still stirring constantly so that nothing sticks to the bottom of the pan. Keep simmering and stirring until the sauce has reached your desired consistency, then remove the pan from the heat.

4. Add the extras (if using) and stir until the cheese has melted into the sauce.

5. Taste and adjust the seasoning with a little more salt if needed. You would only add acid, such as a squeeze of lemon juice, if it tastes heavy and dense and needs something to cut through the sauce to liven it up. If the sauce becomes too thick as it cools, just add a little more non-dairy milk, and if it needs to be thickened, just bring it back to the boil and leave it to reduce for a few more minutes, stirring continuously. Remember that as the sauce cools it also thickens.

RECIPE:	BASIC BÉCHAMEL	CHEESY GARLIC AND BASIL BÉCHAMEL
NON-DAIRY MILK	400ml oat milk	400ml oat milk
FLAVOUR AGENTS AND SEASONING	½ an onion studded with 2 cloves Pinch of freshly ground nutmeg Pinches of salt and freshly ground black pepper	1 tsp garlic powder Pinch of salt
HERBS	1 bay leaf	10g fresh basil leaves, roughly chopped
ROUX	3 tbsp olive oil 3 tbsp plain white flour	3 tbsp olive oil 3 tbsp plain white flour
EXTRAS		3 tbsp grated vegan cheese of choice 1 tbsp nutritional yeast

BREAKDOWN ↑ ↓

CREAMY CASHEW SAUCES

Sometimes you crave something creamy and satisfying, which is where cashews come in – they provide fat and give a sauce that creamy mouthfeel. Try serving the basic cashew cream sauce with spaghetti and vegan bacon (see p. 60) for a vegan take on a classic carbonara.

We recommend serving these sauces with 300g of dried pasta.

RECIPE:	BASIC CASHEW CREAM SAUCE	CREAMY RED PEPPER SAUCE	CREAMY BASIL AND LEMON SAUCE
FAT	100g cashew nuts	100g cashew nuts	100g cashew nuts
EXTRAS		100g roasted red peppers (p. 300)	30g fresh basil, leaves stripped from the stems
NON-DAIRY MILK	500ml oat milk	500ml oat milk	500ml oat milk
ACID	Juice of ½ a lemon	Juice of ½ a lemon	Juice of ½ a lemon
FLAVOUR AGENTS AND SEASONING	1 tsp garlic powder 1 tsp salt	1 tsp garlic powder 1 tsp salt	Zest of 1 lemon 1 tsp garlic powder 1 tsp salt

(left margin: ↑ BREAKDOWN ↓)

Serves 3

1. These sauces couldn't be easier – simply put all the ingredients into a blender and blend until smooth. It might take a little longer if your blender is less powerful, but it's worth giving it the time to ensure the sauce is super smooth.

2. To serve, simply stir the sauce through your hot cooked pasta. If the sauce is too thick, add a little reserved pasta cooking water to loosen it until it reaches your desired consistency, or if the sauce is too thin leave it to cook for a few minutes with the pasta and it will naturally thicken.

CREAMY VEG-BASED SAUCES

Serves 5 to 6

These versatile sauces can be re-created with many starchy veg. It does look better when you use a bright starchy veg such as squash, pumpkin or sweet potato as opposed to a regular potato.

The basis of this sauce is cooking a starch until it becomes soft, then pasta water is added and blended with some olive oil until a creamy, starchy sauce is reached. The best-known example is a squash and sage sauce, which you will see in the framework on p. 180.

We recommend serving these sauces with 200g of dried pasta, which will yield approx. 500g of cooked pasta.

1. Cook the pasta in a large pot of boiling salted water according to the packet instructions, until al dente (and see p. 197). Drain the pasta in a colander set over a separate large pot so that you can reserve all the cooking water.

2. Peel and finely chop the garlic. To prepare the other veg, finely chop the mushrooms or fine beans. Chop the leaves from the fresh herbs.

3. Measure out 275ml of the reserved pasta cooking water and place in a blender along with the cooked starchy veg, garlic, olive oil and salt. Blend until combined into a smooth, creamy sauce. Taste and adjust the seasoning with a little more salt or acid if needed.

4. Heat a splash of olive oil in a frying pan on a high heat. Add the other veg (mushrooms or fine beans) and cook for 5 to 6 minutes, stirring regularly. Once they start to brown around the edges, take the pan off the heat.

5. To serve, simply stir the sauce through your hot cooked pasta, then add the chopped fresh herbs. If the sauce is too thick, add a little of the reserved pasta cooking water to loosen until it reaches your desired consistency. Divide the pasta between wide, shallow bowls, then divide the cooked mushrooms or fine beans on top.

RECIPE:	SQUASH AND SAGE SAUCE	SWEET POTATO AND BASIL SAUCE
DRIED PASTA	200g linguine	200g spaghetti
RESERVED PASTA COOKING WATER	275ml reserved pasta cooking water	275ml reserved pasta cooking water
STARCHY VEG	400g roasted butternut squash (p. 298)	400g roasted sweet potatoes (p. 300)
GARLIC	3 garlic cloves	2 garlic cloves
OLIVE OIL	4 tbsp olive oil, plus extra for cooking	6 tbsp olive oil, plus extra for cooking
SALT	Generous pinch of salt	Generous pinch of salt
OTHER VEG	150g mushrooms	150g fine beans
FRESH HERBS	10g fresh sage leaves	15g fresh basil leaves

BREAKDOWN ↑ ↓

VEGAN CHEESE SAUCES

Serves 1

These sauces are all based on the Italian dish cacio e pepe ('cheese and pepper'), where the sauce is made with just cheese, pasta cooking water and black pepper.

A good trick for adding more flavour to these dishes is to reduce the amount of water you cook the pasta in. Usually the ratio of pasta to water is 1:10, so for example, 100g of pasta would normally be cooked in 1,000ml (1 litre) of water. However, if you cook the pasta in less water – for example, using a 1:5 ratio (100g of pasta cooked in 500ml of water) – it means the pasta cooking water will be more intensely starchy, which will make it easier to form a creamy sauce, and it will be more salty too.

1. Cook the pasta in a large pot of boiling salted water according to the packet instructions until al dente, but first making sure that you work out the 1:5 ratio of pasta to cooking water based on how many portions of pasta you're making (see the recipe intro). Drain the pasta in a colander set over a separate large pot so that you can reserve all the cooking water. Set the pasta aside and continue to boil the pasta water for a further 2 minutes to concentrate the starch.

2. Put the cooked pasta into its original large pot along with the cheese and the herbs or seasoning. Slowly add the reduced pasta water a little at a time until the sauce starts to come together. As you stir, try to bang the pasta off the sides of the pot so that the pasta releases its starch and this creates an emulsion with the melted cheese. A silky-smooth sauce should start to form.

3. Taste and adjust the seasoning with a little more salt if needed, though it will probably be salty enough from the reduced cooking water and the cheese.

4. Stir in the veg (if using), then divide the pasta between wide, shallow bowls and serve straight away, with extra vegan Parmesan on the side for sprinkling over.

RECIPE:	CACIO E PEPE	CHEESY BASIL AND SUN-DRIED TOMATO SAUCE	OLIVE AND GRILLED COURGETTE SAUCE
DRIED PASTA	100g pasta per person	100g pasta per person	100g pasta per person
CHEESE	45g grated vegan Parmesan per person	45g grated vegan Parmesan per person	45g grated vegan Parmesan per person
HERBS OR SEASONING	1 tsp freshly ground black pepper per person	10g fresh basil leaves per person	½ sprig of fresh thyme per person
VEG		30g sun-blushed tomatoes per person	20g pitted olives per person (our fave is Kalamata) 30g sliced grilled courgette per person

← BREAKDOWN →

LASAGNE

Serves 6

There are infinite variations on lasagne that can be made depending on what veg or sauces you use, but the essential components tend to be the same:

- **Tomato-based sauce:** This is usually a rich ragù or tomato-based sauce (see p. 171). Our framework uses 1 litre of tomato sauce.

- **Béchamel sauce:** We use 500ml of béchamel (aka white sauce – see p. 175). If you want to make your white sauce even richer and more indulgent, add more olive oil or use some creamy cashew sauce (see p. 177).

- **Veg:** We usually bake 1kg to 1.2kg of veg for a lasagne, then stir the cooked veg into the tomato sauce for a more traditional lasagne or through most of the béchamel sauce for a white lasagne.

- **Lasagne sheets:** You can use 500g of either wholemeal or white dried lasagne sheets. Wholemeal lasagne sheets have more fibre than white, but they are darker in colour and will change the traditional appearance of the dish. They will also take longer to cook. White dried lasagne sheets are the most common, plus they taste great and cook quicker than wholemeal lasagne sheets.

We've provided recipes for two variations of lasagne that can be easily adapted. For example, in the traditional lasagne the mushrooms could be swapped for fine beans or fennel, while in the white lasagne you could use sweet potatoes or pumpkin instead of squash. The first recipe is for a more traditional lasagne, with a spicy tomato sauce packed full of veg and topped with a smooth béchamel. The second recipe is for a white lasagne, as the entire lasagne is based on a béchamel sauce that's infused with lemon zest and mint, giving it a lighter feeling and a fresh taste.

1. Preheat the oven to 180°C fan/400°F/gas 6.

2. Finely chop your veg, then drizzle with the oil and salt, tossing to coat. Spread out on two baking trays, ensuring the veg have enough room between them – if they're too close together they'll steam instead of roast. Bake in the preheated oven for 30 minutes.

3. Stir the cooked veg and optional extras through the main sauce of your dish – the tomato sauce if making the traditional lasagne or the béchamel sauce for the white lasagne. If you're making the white lasagne, set aside 500ml of the béchamel before you add the veg to the rest. Make sure the veg sauce is nice and thick, otherwise the lasagne won't hold its shape when you serve it. If it's too thin, add some more cooked starchy veg, such as sweet potatoes or potatoes, pumpkin or squash. Taste and adjust the seasoning with a little more salt if needed.

4. **To layer up the traditional lasagne:**

   Put a thin layer of béchamel sauce on the bottom of a large ovenproof baking dish or lasagne dish, spreading it out evenly. Add a single even layer of dried lasagne sheets. Next add a layer of your tomato and veg sauce and a layer of baby spinach (if using as a further optional extra), then put another layer of lasagne sheets on top. Repeat with one more layer of tomato and veg sauce and baby spinach (if using), then a final layer of lasagne sheets. Spread the remaining béchamel sauce on top, ensuring the lasagne sheets are completely covered by the béchamel (this will stop them drying out while baking). Sprinkle the grated vegan cheese over the top (if using).

   To layer up the white lasagne:

   Add half the reserved béchamel sauce without the veg in a thin layer on the bottom of a large ovenproof baking dish or lasagne dish, spreading it out evenly. Add a single even layer of dried lasagne sheets. Next add half the béchamel and veg sauce, then put another layer of lasagne sheets on top. Repeat with the remaining half of the béchamel and veg sauce, then a final layer of lasagne sheets. Lastly, spread the remaining béchamel sauce without the veg on top, ensuring the lasagne sheets are completely covered by the béchamel (this will stop them drying out while baking). Sprinkle the grated vegan cheese over the top (if using).

$\rightarrow$

5. Bake in the preheated oven for 20 to 25 minutes, until the lasagne sheets are cooked and the dish is bubbling. To test, simply insert a knife or skewer into the middle of the dish – it should pass through the pasta easily. If it's not cooked yet, turn the heat down so that the top doesn't brown too much and cook until the pasta sheets are soft.

6. Remove the lasagne from the oven and garnish with fresh basil or parsley (if using). The easiest way to cut lasagne is with scissors, as it stops you having to chase lasagne sheets around a messy dish. You probably think this sounds silly, but as soon as you try it, you'll understand!

RECIPE:	TRADITIONAL LASAGNE	WHITE LASAGNE
VEG	1kg mixed veg, such as mushrooms, peppers, courgettes and aubergines 1 tbsp oil 1 tsp salt	1.2kg mixed veg, such as butternut squash, leeks, fine beans and frozen peas 1 tbsp oil 1 tsp salt
TOMATO SAUCE	1 batch of simple spicy chilli and garlic tomato sauce (p. 173)	
BÉCHAMEL SAUCE	1 batch of basic béchamel (p. 175)	3 batches of basic béchamel (p. 175)
DRIED LASAGNE SHEETS	500g dried lasagne sheets	500g dried lasagne sheets
OPTIONAL EXTRAS	Zest of 1 lemon A few handfuls of baby spinach	Zest of 2 lemons Juice of 1 lemon 15g fresh mint, finely chopped
CHEESE (OPTIONAL)	50g to 100g grated vegan cheese	50g to 100g grated vegan cheese
GARNISH	Fresh basil leaves or chopped fresh flat-leaf parsley	

← **BREAKDOWN** →

CANNELLONI

Cannelloni is a tube-like type of pasta that means 'large reeds' in Italian. It's generally stuffed with a filling and baked in a sauce. The most common filling for cannelloni is spinach and ricotta, so we've re-created this popular version using a simple homemade vegan ricotta.

The basic ratio for cannelloni is 500g of filling to 500ml of sauce. Your stuffed cannelloni can be baked in a tomato sauce or a béchamel sauce, depending on which you prefer, but it's usually baked in a tomato sauce and then topped with a cheese or béchamel sauce. We like to add a double layer of filled cannelloni tubes in the baking tray, as we find this to be more substantial and satisfying, equivalent to a slice of lasagne. Plus if you use just one layer, the tubes might shrink during baking.

The easiest way to fill your cannelloni is to use scissors to cut the panel off one side of the box, then turn the box so that the tubes are all facing up. Fill a piping bag or a ziplock bag with a corner snipped off with your filling, and fill each of the tubes. Make sure to give them a light tap on the worktop to compact the filling and ensure that they are all completely filled, otherwise they might not cook properly.

Another point to note is that your filling should be sufficiently thick but also super smooth. It needs to be thick so that it won't leak out of the pasta tube, but not so thick that you can't squeeze it out of the piping bag. If it's too thick, just add a little water to loosen it or a splash of oil for extra richness. The filling also needs to be perfectly smooth, otherwise lumps can get caught in your piping bag.

Serves 5 to 6

Preheat the oven to 200°C fan/425°F/gas 7.

Spinach and ricotta cannelloni:

1. To make the vegan ricotta filling, soak the cashews in a bowl of cold water overnight (or if you don't have time, boil them for 10 minutes). Drain and rinse the soaked cashews, then put them into a blender with the 200ml of fresh water, the garlic powder and the salt and blend until super smooth.

2. Put the spinach into a small saucepan and pour over 50ml of just-boiled water from the kettle, then cover the pan with a lid and set aside for 3 minutes, until all the leaves have wilted down. Pour the spinach into a colander set in the sink, then give it a good squeeze to remove any excess moisture. Add to the vegan ricotta and stir to mix well.

3. Spoon the filling into a piping bag or a ziplock bag with one corner snipped off and fill the pasta tubes, making sure they're all completely filled (see the note in the introduction).

Roasted red pepper pesto cannelloni:

1. Cut the potatoes into bite-size pieces, then place in a saucepan, cover with lightly salted cold water and bring to the boil. Reduce the heat to a simmer and cook for 10 minutes, until cooked through and tender.

2. Drain well, then put the potatoes back into the hot pan for a few minutes to remove any excess moisture. Transfer to a bowl and mash until super smooth, then stir in the pesto. Taste and adjust the seasoning with a little salt if needed.

3. Spoon the filling into a piping bag or a ziplock bag with one corner snipped off and fill the pasta tubes, making sure they're all completely filled (see the note in the introduction).

Sweet potato and basil cannelloni:

1. Put the roasted sweet potatoes, basil pesto and a squeeze of lemon juice into a large bowl and mash until super smooth. Taste and adjust the seasoning with a little salt if needed.

2. Spoon the filling into a piping bag or a ziplock bag with one corner snipped off and fill the pasta tubes, making sure they're all completely filled (see the note in the introduction).

To assemble:

1. Put two layers of the filled pasta tubes into a baking dish. Pour over your sauce, ensuring all the tubes are covered in sauce so that the pasta doesn't dry out while baking. Top with grated vegan cheese and bake for 20 to 25 minutes in the preheated oven, until bubbling.

2. Test to ensure that the pasta is fully cooked. Insert a fork and if it slides in effortlessly the pasta is cooked, if not, turn the temperature down to 150°C fan/325°F/gas 3 and continue cooking until the pasta is soft.

RECIPE:	SPINACH AND RICOTTA CANNELLONI	ROASTED RED PEPPER PESTO CANNELLONI	SWEET POTATO AND BASIL CANNELLONI
FILLING	350g cashews 200ml water ⅓ tsp garlic powder Pinch of salt 200g baby spinach	150g potato 300g roasted red pepper pesto (p. 167) Pinch of salt (optional)	300g roasted sweet potato (p. 300) 200g basil pesto (p. 167) Lemon juice, to taste Pinch of salt (optional)
DRIED PASTA	2 × 250g boxes of cannelloni	2 × 250g boxes of cannelloni	2 × 250g boxes of cannelloni
SAUCE	500ml simple spicy chilli and garlic tomato sauce (p. 173)	500ml simple spicy chilli and garlic tomato sauce (p. 173)	500ml basic béchamel sauce (p. 175)
CHEESE	100g vegan Cheddar or Parmesan cheese, grated	100g vegan Cheddar or Parmesan cheese, grated	100g vegan Cheddar or Parmesan cheese, grated

BREAKDOWN

PASTA BAKE

Serves 4

A pasta bake is always a crowd-pleaser. We served many variations of this for years in the café and people always loved it. The basic idea is to use a smaller pasta, such as penne or fusilli, serve it with a lovely tomato or béchamel sauce with some sort of fat added in the form of nuts, seeds or oil, stir in some roasted veg, then top with vegan cheese or breadcrumbs and bake in the oven until bubbling.

1.   Preheat the oven to 200°C fan/425°F/gas 7.

2.   Cook the pasta in a large pot of boiling salted water according to the packet instructions, until al dente (and see p. 197). Drain and rinse in cold water to stop it cooking any further.

3.   Put the sauce and fat into a large bowl and stir to combine, then taste and adjust the seasoning if needed. Stir in the roasted veg and the cooked pasta, then transfer to a large baking dish and level it out.

4.   To make the topping, strip the thyme leaves from their stalks (if using). Mix the breadcrumbs with the nuts (if using), then add the oil and a pinch of salt. Scatter evenly on top of the pasta.

5.   Bake in the preheated oven for 20 minutes, until bubbling and the topping is golden brown. Bring the dish straight to the table and let everyone help themselves.

→

RECIPE:	BASIL AND ROASTED VEG PASTA BAKE	CREAMY MUSHROOM AND LEEK PASTA BAKE	CHEESY SWEET POTATO AND PINE NUT PASTA BAKE
DRIED PASTA	250g fusilli	250g penne	250g farfalle
SAUCE	500ml spicy tomato sauce (p. 173)	500ml béchamel sauce (p. 175)	500ml spicy tomato sauce (p. 173)
FAT	250g basil pesto (p. 167)	100g vegan cheese 50ml olive oil	200g vegan cheese
SEASONING (TO TASTE)	Salt and freshly ground black pepper	Salt and freshly ground black pepper	Salt and freshly ground black pepper
ROASTED VEG	500g mix of roasted peppers, aubergines and courgettes (pp. 298–300)	250g roasted leeks (p. 300) 250g roasted mushrooms (p. 300)	500g roasted sweet potatoes (p. 300)
TOPPING	100g dried breadcrumbs 50ml olive oil 3 sprigs of fresh thyme	100g flaked almonds 50g dried breadcrumbs 50ml olive oil	100g pine nuts 100g flaked almonds 50g dried breadcrumbs 50ml olive oil

BREAKDOWN

THE BASICS FOR COOKING PASTA

There are many myths and a lot of confusion about the best way to cook pasta. After spending a lot of time with an Italian friend, Pietro, in Rome, we learned how to cook pasta the authentic Italian way. (Having said that, though, this is of course a vegan cookbook, so if we've deviated from some of the rules and are flying in the face of your Italian nonna's recipe, it's not intentional! We're a little rebellious by nature and we need to bring in flavour from different areas other than the traditional Italian ones.)

In Italian cookbooks, the ratio of pasta to water is often 1:10, so if you're cooking 100g of dried pasta, you should cook it in 1,000ml (1 litre) of water. This means there will be enough room for the pasta to cook properly and not stick together.

- First boil the kettle or fill the pot three-quarters full with water and bring to the boil.

- Add enough salt to the water that it has a salinity similar to seawater. A good rule of thumb is to use 1 tablespoon of salt per litre of water. This might sound like a crazy amount of salt, but don't worry, most of it will end up being washed down the drain and a crucial amount will remain to adequately season the pasta. It will also give more buoyancy to the water, which means the pasta is less likely to stick together.

- Don't add oil to the pasta cooking water. The oil will simply float on the surface of the water, then coat the pasta as you drain it. This will form a layer between the pasta and the sauce and make the sauce less likely to stick to the pasta. The pasta itself is very starchy, so most sauces will naturally want to stick to it, but if the pasta has been coated with oil it will act as a lubricant, making the sauce more likely to slide off the pasta. Using a large pot and plenty of salt will go a long way towards keeping your pasta from sticking together, but you could also give it a stir every now and then with a long wooden spoon.

- Cook the pasta how you like it. In Italy pasta is always cooked al dente, which translates as 'to the tooth'. This means that it's slightly undercooked and firm and still has a little bite to it – it shouldn't be super soft and squidgy. We usually cook our pasta for 1 minute less than what the packet instructions say, then taste some to test how done it is. But like anything, you should cook your pasta how you like it. In Ireland we seem to like our pasta on the mushy side and tend to overcook it, which the Italians would get very upset about, but to each their own!

Stews, Curries, Noodles and One-Pot Wonders

These heart-warming dinners are some of our favourite types of dishes. Whether you're making a stew or a curry, a slow-cooking dinner or a quick 10-minute midweek supper, the same essential principles and frameworks apply.

THE ESSENTIALS

Base veg: The base veg for stews, curries and meals in minutes is usually some combination of onions or spring onions (or if you want to be a little fancy, pearl onions or shallots), garlic, ginger and chilli. You may be less likely to use any ginger or chilli in stews, but for curries and coconut-based dishes you will use all four of the above (sometimes known as an 'Indian stock'). Simply cook the peeled and diced base veg in 1 or 2 tablespoons of oil on a high heat for 3 to 4 minutes, until the veg start to brown. Browning is an indicator of flavour development and caramelization, which is what you want here.

Core veg: The core veg you use will have one of the biggest impacts on the cooking time of your dish. Aim for 700g to 750g of vegetables in total. In the template on p. 205 we say 25% for simplicity, but you can add more if you want.

If you want your dinner to be a fast-cooking midweek dinner, then choose fast-cooking veg, such as courgettes, mushrooms, pak choi, peppers, spinach, spring onions, sugar snap peas, mangetout or green beans.

Finely chop your fast-cooking veg, add to the base with a generous pinch of salt, and cook for a few minutes on a high heat, stirring regularly. The nice thing about most fast-cooking veg is that nearly all of them can be eaten raw or with a bit of crunch, which makes them perfect for quick dinners.

Veg that take longer to cook and are therefore better suited to stews or slower-cooked one-pot wonders are aubergines, cauliflower, potatoes, root veg (such as carrots, parsnips and turnips), squash, sweet potatoes or pumpkin.

For a stew we usually chop 600g to 700g of these longer-cooking veg into bite-size pieces, then add them to the cooked base along with a good pinch of salt. Turn the heat down to medium, cover with a lid and sweat for 10 to 15 minutes, remembering to stir occasionally. Alternatively, you can bake these longer-cooking veg on a baking tray in an oven preheated to 180°C fan/400°F/gas 6 for 25 minutes with 1 tablespoon of oil and a pinch of salt, tossing to coat.

Beans and legumes: We add tinned beans, lentils or chickpeas to the vast majority of our stews, curries and fast-cooking dinners. They are such a good way of bulking out a dish and adding more bite, substance and texture while adding loads of nutrition too. Beans are high in fibre and protein and are mostly made up of complex carbohydrates, so they are great for energy.

We generally use tinned beans at home, as they are so easy and practical, but in our cafés and commercial kitchens we soak and cook dried beans (see p. 302 for more information on how to cook dried beans from scratch). We usually use 500g of tinned beans (2 × 400g tins of beans after they have been drained and rinsed). Use whatever beans you like or that best fit the type of dish you are making. The

ones we use most often are black beans, butter beans, cannellini beans, chickpeas, kidney beans and lentils.

Liquid: The liquid ingredients are the base of your dish and this is where a lot of the flavour comes from. In many cases, what turns a good dish into a great dish is the cooking liquid. Classic French cooking requires reducing the liquid for long periods of time to develop and concentrate flavour, but you can make a super-tasty sauce in minutes instead of hours!

Your liquid ingredients should make up approx. 35% of your dish, but there will be some times when slightly less is needed and others when it needs slightly more. For simplicity the framework on p. 205 says that 25% to 35% of your dish is liquid, but realistically it's more like 40%, as we base it around the volume of tins.

- Coconut milk-based sauce: Coconut milk works well in Asian-style dishes such as curries, dahls, noodle dishes, etc. It adds a satiating and super-creamy element to a sauce with a subtle sweetness and marries well with spices. Coconut milk is naturally high in fat, most of which is saturated fat. Full-fat coconut milk is typically about 20% fat, whereas low-fat coconut milk is typically around 9% (they just reduce the amount of coconut cream at the top of the tin). Due to the high saturated fat content, you should limit the amount of coconut milk-based sauces you consume to a couple of times a week if you are focused on health.

- Tomato-based sauce: Tomato-based sauces are great for Mexican chilli, stews, one-pot casseroles and, of course, pasta dishes. We tend to use tinned chopped tomatoes, some tomato purée (to add some sweetness and body to the sauce) and a little sweetener (maple syrup) to balance the natural acidity of the tomatoes and seasoning. For a Mexican chilli, for example, we use chilli powder, ground cumin, ground coriander, smoked paprika, salt and ground black pepper, with some lime juice as acid to give vibrancy and some chopped coriander to give freshness.

- Nut butter/tahini emulsion: To make a creamy sauce, blend some nut butter (such as almond or peanut butter or tahini) with some water or veg stock, spices and seasoning. The nut butter will add body, fat and more satiation to the sauce. We usually season it with some tamari or soy sauce, freshly squeezed lime juice, spices such as ground ginger for a little heat and maybe some sweetener too. This type of sauce works well for a satay-type dish or curry.

- **Stock, broth or gravy for stew:** The liquid in a stew will reduce as it cooks. It will also thicken from the starches that are released from the veg and beans. If you're using root veg in a stew, the sauce can be thinner going in at the start, as it will thicken as you cook out the starches in the root veg. Alternatively, you can add a roux to thicken a sauce (see p. 175). The liquid in a stew can include:

> Water
> Veg stock
> Bean broth
> Wine
> Tinned tomatoes
> Thickeners, such as cornflour, rice flour, tapioca starch, arrowroot, etc.
> Flavour agents, such as tamari or soy sauce, nutritional yeast, spices and seasoning

Once you add your liquid to the stew, bring it to the boil, then cover the pan, reduce the heat and cook at a gentle simmer until the veg are soft and tender and almost melt in your mouth.

Flavour agents: The flavour agents are the core flavours that make one type of dish stand out from another. They are the flavour notes that differentiate a Brazilian feijoada or a French ratatouille from a Moroccan tagine. Each will have its own subtle nuances that will be based around the five flavours: salty, bitter, sweet, sour and umami. For more details on flavour agents, seasoning and spices, check out pp. 11–14.

Garnish: Stews, curries and one-pot dishes are delicious, but they can sometimes look a bit drab. All they need is a generous garnish to brighten them up. See p. 17 for a list of some of the garnishes we use most often.

STEW

This highly flexible framework can expand and contract if you want to include more veg, beans, etc. A stew will typically take a while to cook, so we usually use slower-cooking veg. To cook all these dishes in half the time, simply use fast-cooking veg (see the list on p. 200) and spring onions instead of onions.

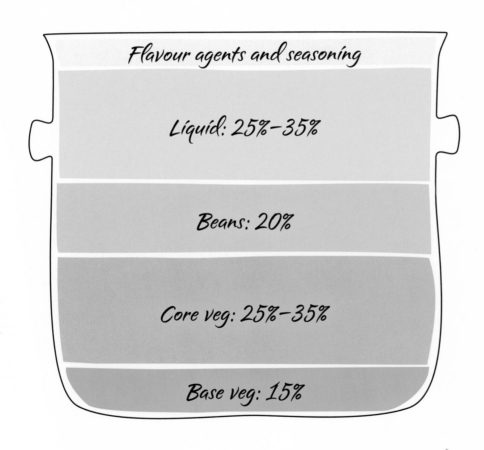

Flavour agents and seasoning

Liquid: 25%–35%

Beans: 20%

Core veg: 25%–35%

Base veg: 15%

Serves 5

1. Peel and finely chop your base veg into even-sized pieces, including deseeding the chilli (if using). Peel and chop the core veg into bite-size pieces. Drain and rinse the chickpeas, beans or lentils.

2. Heat the oil in a large saucepan on a high heat. Fry the sausages (if using) before you add the base veg to get a lovely char on them, ensuring they are cooked through, then transfer to a plate and set aside.

3. Add the base veg to the pan, then reduce the heat to medium and cook for 3 to 5 minutes, until the onions start to brown.

4. Add the core veg and spices (if using) to the pan along with a generous pinch of salt. Cover the pan with a lid and cook for 10 to 15 minutes, until soft and nearly cooked through, stirring occasionally to stop the veg sticking to the bottom of the pan and burning. If you're using faster-cooking veg, this may take only 5 minutes.

5. Put the charred sausages (if using) back into the pan (slice them before adding them) along with the drained and rinsed chickpeas, beans or lentils, liquid, flavour agents and seasoning. Bring to the boil, then reduce to a simmer and cook for 10 minutes (or longer if you would like a thicker sauce).

6. Taste and adjust the seasoning with a little more salt, pepper, acid or heat if needed. Divide between five bowls, garnish and serve.

RECIPE:	MOROCCAN ALMOND, CHICKPEA AND TOMATO STEW	BRAZILIAN FEIJOADA	FRENCH WHITE BEAN AND LEMON CASSOULET	NEW ORLEANS GUMBO	RATATOUILLE WITH LENTILS
BASE VEG	2 medium onions (250g) 3 garlic cloves 1 fresh red chilli 1 × thumb-size piece of fresh ginger 1 to 2 tbsp oil	2 medium onions (250g) 3 garlic cloves 1 fresh red chilli, deseeded 1 to 2 tbsp oil	1 large or 2 medium leeks (350g) 3 garlic cloves 1 to 2 tbsp oil	2 medium onions (250g) 3 garlic cloves 1 to 2 tbsp oil	2 medium onions (250g) 3 garlic cloves 1 to 2 tbsp oil
CORE VEG	250g aubergine 200g peppers 200g courgette	6 vegan sausages (thawed if using frozen or see p. 64) 200g sweet potatoes 200g peppers	3 vegan sausages (thawed if using frozen or see p. 64) 2 medium carrots ½ a celeriac (400g)	6 vegan sausages (thawed if using frozen or see p. 64) 250g okra, squash or sweet potatoes 200g yellow peppers	250g courgette 250g aubergine 200g peppers
SPICES	1½ tsp ground cumin 1 tsp ground coriander 1 tsp smoked paprika	2 tsp ground coriander 1 tsp smoked paprika		1 tbsp paprika 1 tsp chilli powder	

RECIPES AND BREAKDOWN CONTINUE ON OPPOSITE PAGE

↑ BREAKDOWN ↓

RECULUE: *CONTINUED*	MOROCCAN ALMOND, CHICKPEA AND TOMATO STEW	BRAZILIAN FEIJOADA	FRENCH WHITE BEAN AND LEMON CASSOULET	NEW ORLEANS GUMBO	RATATOUILLE WITH LENTILS
CHICKPEAS, BEANS OR LENTILS	2 × 400g tins of chickpeas	2 × 400g tins of black beans	2 × 400g tins of cannellini or butter beans	2 × 400g tins of black-eyed beans	2 × 400g tins of lentils
LIQUID	1 × 400g tin of chopped tomatoes 400ml veg stock	800ml veg stock	800ml veg stock (use extra stock here because the wine evaporates) 250ml white wine	1 × 400g tin of chopped tomatoes 400ml veg stock	1 × 400g tin of chopped tomatoes 400ml veg stock
FLAVOUR AGENTS	Juice of 1 lemon or lime 20g dried apricots, diced 1 bunch of fresh mint or parsley, leaves picked 2 tbsp tamari or soy sauce	Juice of 2 limes 2 bay leaves 1½ tbsp tamari ½ tsp dried thyme	Zest of ½ a lemon 8 sprigs of fresh thyme 2 bay leaves	Juice of 1 lime 2 bay leaves 2 tbsp tamari or soy sauce	6 sprigs of fresh thyme 1 tbsp maple syrup 2 tsp balsamic vinegar
SEASONING (TO TASTE)	1 tsp salt	1 tsp salt ½ tsp freshly ground black pepper	2 tsp salt ¼ tsp freshly ground black pepper	1 tsp salt 1 tsp freshly ground black pepper	2 tsp salt
GARNISH	Chopped fresh flat-leaf parsley Chopped fresh mint Flaked almonds	Fresh coriander leaves Lime zest and squeeze of juice	Fresh thyme leaves Chopped fresh flat-leaf parsley	Thinly sliced spring onions	Fresh basil leaves

CURRY

These curries can be cooked quickly for an easy midweek dinner or using slower-cooking veg when you have more time (see the list on p. 200). We use a wide-bottomed pan for cooking our curries, as there is more surface area to brown the veg and because it also cooks quicker and the flavours come together better.

Spices, flavour agents and seasoning

Liquid: 40%

Beans/protein: 25%

Core veg: 20%–25%

Base veg: 10%

→

Serves 4

1. To prepare the base veg, peel and finely chop the onions and garlic or thinly slice the spring onions. Deseed the chilli and finely chop. Peel and grate the ginger.

2. Peel and chop the core veg into bite-size pieces. Drain and rinse the beans (if using).

3. Heat the oil in a large saucepan on a high heat. If using tofu or tempeh, slice it into small bite-size pieces and cook for 5 to 8 minutes until it is slightly golden on each side. Remove from the pan and set aside. Add the base veg to the pan, then reduce the heat to medium and cook for 2 to 4 minutes, stirring occasionally, until the onions or spring onions start to brown.

4. Add the core veg and spices to the pan along with a generous pinch of salt. Cover the pan with a lid and cook for 10 to 15 minutes (or 20 minutes for the aubergines and potatoes if you're making the Bombay tomato curry), until soft and nearly cooked through, stirring occasionally to stop the veg sticking to the bottom of the pan and burning. If you're using faster-cooking veg, this may take only 5 minutes. In the case of the Bombay tomato curry, if it's starting to stick to the bottom of the pan, add a couple of tablespoons of water to deglaze the pan, scraping up any caramelized bits from the bottom of the pan with a wooden spoon.

5. Add your drained and rinsed beans (if using), liquid, flavour agents and seasoning. If you're making the Indonesian satay, blend all the liquid ingredients together first before adding them to the pan. Bring to the boil, then reduce to a simmer and cook for 10 to 15 minutes (or longer if you would like a thicker sauce).

6. Taste and adjust the seasoning with a little more salt, pepper, acid or heat if needed. Divide between four warmed bowls, garnish and serve.

RECIPE:	CHICKPEA, MUSHROOM AND FINE BEANS CURRY	ALOO GOBI (CREAMY INDIAN CAULIFLOWER AND POTATO CURRY)	CHANA MASALA	INDONESIAN SATAY	BOMBAY TOMATO CURRY
BASE VEG	4 spring onions 2 garlic cloves ½ fresh red chilli ½ × thumb-size piece of fresh ginger 1 to 2 tbsp oil	4 spring onions 3 garlic cloves 1 fresh red chilli ½ × thumb-size piece of fresh ginger 1 to 2 tbsp oil	1 medium onion 3 garlic cloves 1 fresh red chilli ½ × thumb-size piece of fresh ginger 1 to 2 tbsp oil	2 medium onions 2 garlic cloves ½ fresh red chilli ½ × thumb-size piece of fresh ginger 1 to 2 tbsp oil	2 medium onions 3 garlic cloves 1 fresh red chilli ½ × thumb-size piece of fresh ginger 1 to 2 tbsp oil
CORE VEG	200g mushrooms 100g fine beans or sugar snap peas	1 head of cauliflower, roasted (p. 298) 250g potatoes	300g sweet potatoes 100g green beans or sugar snap peas	300g sweet potatoes	1 aubergine 400g potatoes
SPICES	1 tbsp curry powder 1 tsp paprika 1 tsp ground cumin 1 tsp ground coriander	1½ tbsp black mustard seeds 1 tbsp ground turmeric 1 tbsp cumin seeds 1 tsp garam masala	1 tsp ground cumin 1 tsp ground coriander 1 tsp garam masala ½ tsp ground turmeric	1 tsp ground cumin 1 tsp ground coriander 1 tsp ground cinnamon	1½ tsp salt 1 tsp ground cumin 1 tsp ground coriander 1 tsp fennel seeds ½ tsp ground cardamom ½ tsp ground turmeric

BREAKDOWN → **↓**

RECIPES AND BREAKDOWN CONTINUE ON OPPOSITE PAGE

RECITE: CONTINUED	CHICKPEA, MUSHROOM AND FINE BEANS CURRY	ALOO GOBI (CREAMY INDIAN CAULIFLOWER AND POTATO CURRY)	CHANA MASALA	INDONESIAN SATAY	BOMBAY TOMATO CURRY
BEANS, TOFU OR TEMPEH	2 × 400g tins of chickpeas		1 × 400g tin of chickpeas	300g tempeh or tofu	
LIQUID	1 × 400g tin of chopped tomatoes 1 × 400ml tin of coconut milk	1 × 400ml tin of coconut milk 400ml veg stock	1 × 400g tin of chopped tomatoes 1 × 400ml tin of coconut milk	800ml veg stock 4 tbsp almond butter 2 tbsp maple syrup 2 tbsp apple cider vinegar	1 × 400g tin of chopped tomatoes 400ml veg stock
FLAVOUR AGENTS	Juice of 1 lemon 1 tbsp tamari or soy sauce	Juice of ½ a lemon 2 tbsp tamari or soy sauce	2 tbsp tamari or soy sauce	Juice of 1 lime 2 tbsp tamari or soy sauce	Juice of ½ lime 2 tbsp maple syrup
SEASONING (TO TASTE)	Salt and freshly ground black pepper Chilli flakes	Salt and freshly ground black pepper Chilli flakes	Salt and freshly ground black pepper Chilli flakes	Salt and freshly ground black pepper Chilli flakes	Salt and freshly ground black pepper Chilli flakes
GARNISH	Finely chopped fresh coriander	Fresh coriander leaves Coconut yoghurt	Dukkah (p. 310)	Beansprouts or toasted nuts (p. 301) Chopped fresh herbs	Flaked almonds Chopped fresh coriander

BREAKDOWN CONTINUED ↑ ↓

FANCIER CURRY

Serves 3 to 6

Here is a framework for three authentic curries that are more complex in flavour and use more spices, when you have a little more time to play. All three recipes are from our friend Santan, from Goa, who taught them to us. We changed the method to make them quicker and more accessible, but they are just as delicious as his versions. Vindaloo is the spiciest of all curries, but you can easily adjust the recipe to make it milder.

1. Preheat the oven to 200°C fan/425°F/gas 7.

2. Peel and finely chop the base veg, including deseeding the chillies (if using). Set aside.

3. Peel and chop the core veg into bite-size pieces, then put on a baking tray (there's no need to cook the tinned chickpeas if you're making the Goan korma – simply drain and rinse, then set aside). Drizzle with the oil and season with a pinch of salt, then toss to coat. Bake in the preheated oven for 20 minutes, until soft.

4. Meanwhile, toast the whole spices, including the cinnamon stick, cardamom pods and whole cloves (if using), in a hot dry pan for about 5 minutes, until they start to pop. Tip out into a bowl and set aside.

5. Heat the tablespoon of oil in a large saucepan on a high heat. Add the chopped base veg and cook for 3 to 5 minutes, until they start to brown.

6. If you're making the Goan korma, boil the extra veg (the carrots and peppers) for about 10 minutes, until soft, then drain.

7. Put the cooked base veg, liquid, herbs and all the spices into a blender and blend until smooth. If you're making the Goan korma, add the boiled carrots and peppers to the blender too and blend until smooth.

8. Remove the core veg from the oven and add to the saucepan along with the blended sauce (and the chickpeas if you're making the Goan korma). Bring to the boil, then reduce to a simmer and cook for 5 to 10 minutes, until the flavours have infused the sauce, the spices are nicely balanced and the sauce has thickened to your desired consistency.

9. Taste and adjust the seasoning with more salt, acid and pepper if needed, then ladle into warmed bowls, garnish and serve.

RECIPE:	PUMPKIN AND CORIANDER CURRY SERVES 2 TO 3	HOT VINDALOO WITH POTATO AND PEPPER SERVES 2 TO 3	TRADITIONAL GOAN KORMA SERVES 4 TO 6
BASE VEG	2 red onions 4 garlic cloves 2 fresh red chillies 1 × thumb-size piece of fresh ginger 1 tbsp oil	2 red onions 3 garlic cloves 1 × thumb-size piece of fresh ginger 1 tbsp oil	4 small white onions 3 garlic cloves 1 × thumb-size piece of fresh ginger 1 tbsp oil
CORE VEG	250g pumpkin 250g cauliflower 1 tbsp oil Pinch of salt	250g potato 1 aubergine 1 tbsp oil Pinch of salt	2 × 400g tins of chickpeas 1 large cauliflower (approx. 500g) 1 tbsp oil Pinch of salt
SPICES	5 whole cloves 2 or 3 green cardamom pods 1 cinnamon stick 1 tbsp poppy seeds 1½ tsp cumin seeds	10 whole cloves 10 black peppercorns 1 cinnamon stick 3 to 4 tbsp chilli powder 1 tsp ground turmeric Pinch of ground nutmeg	3 tbsp desiccated coconut 3 tbsp curry powder 2 tbsp ground almonds 1 tbsp ground coriander 1 tsp garam masala 1 tsp ground cumin 1 tsp salt ½ tsp ground turmeric

BREAKDOWN

RECIPES AND BREAKDOWN CONTINUE ON OPPOSITE PAGE

RECISE: CONTINUED	PUMPKIN AND CORIANDER CURRY	HOT VINDALOO WITH POTATO AND PEPPER	TRADITIONAL GOAN KORMA
EXTRA VEG			2 carrots ½ red pepper ½ yellow pepper
LIQUID	1 × 400ml tin of coconut milk 100ml veg stock	100ml water 50ml apple cider vinegar 1½ tbsp liquid sweetener	1 × 400g tin of tomatoes 1 × 400ml tin of coconut milk 2 tbsp maple syrup
HERBS	100g fresh coriander		
SEASONING (TO TASTE)	Salt and freshly ground black pepper	Salt and freshly ground black pepper	Salt and freshly ground black pepper
GARNISH	Toasted flaked almonds (p. 301) Ground pink peppercorns Drizzle of dairy-free yoghurt	Fresh coriander leaves Coconut yoghurt with finely diced cucumber	Toasted cashews (p. 301) Chopped fresh flat-leaf parsley

BREAKDOWN CONTINUED

NOODLES

Noodles are fab in a curry and make them more filling. We tend to cook the noodles separately, then incorporate them into the dish so that they absorb the flavours of the sauce rather than simply serving the curry on a bed of noodles.

There are so many different types of noodles on the market now, such as black bean noodles or lentil-based noodles, that are higher in protein, gluten free, etc. Try a few to see which ones you like best, but we usually use 'wholefood' or wholegrain-based noodles, such as wholewheat noodles, brown rice noodles or buckwheat noodles (the latter two are gluten free), as they are more nutritious and have more fibre than noodles made with white flour.

Noodles often come in dried nests that are approx. 50g each, which is one serving, so as a general rule we use 200g of dried noodles to serve 4 people.

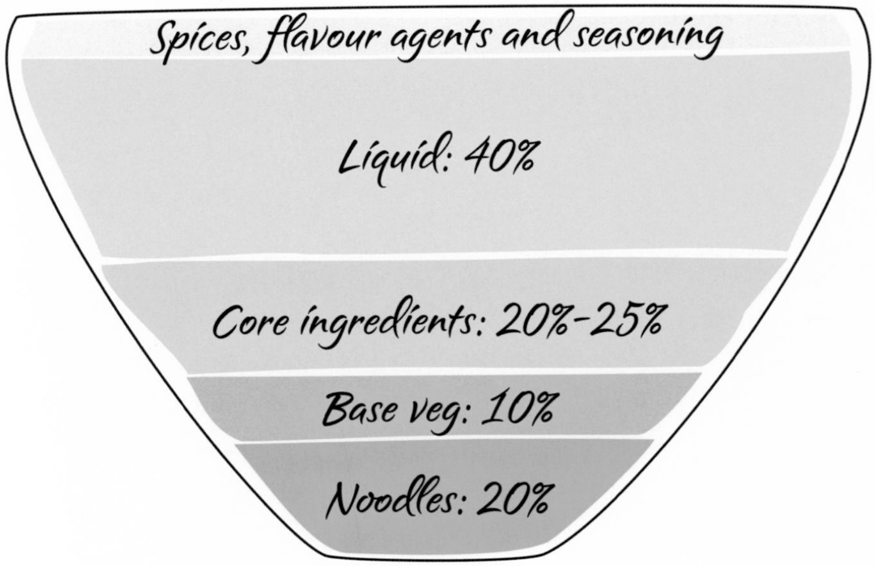

Spices, flavour agents and seasoning

Liquid: 40%

Core ingredients: 20%-25%

Base veg: 10%

Noodles: 20%

$\rightarrow$

Serves 4

1. Cook the noodles in a pot of boiling salted water as per the packet instructions, then drain in a colander and rinse in cold water to stop them sticking together. Set aside.

2. Peel and finely chop the base veg, including deseeding the chilli. Peel and chop the core ingredients into bite-size pieces. However, if you're making the Japanese umami miso ramen, peel the carrot into ribbons instead.

3. Heat the oil in a large saucepan on a high heat. If you're making the sesame and ginger satay, add the tofu or tempeh to the pan and cook for 4 to 5 minutes, stirring regularly, until it starts to sear and turn golden on each side. Transfer to a plate and set aside.

4. Add the chopped base veg, then reduce the heat to medium and cook for 2 to 4 minutes, until the onions or spring onions are starting to brown.

5. Add the chopped core ingredients (including the seared tofu or tempeh, if using), spices and a generous pinch of salt to the pan. Cover the pan with a lid and cook for 10 to 15 minutes, until soft and nearly cooked through, stirring occasionally to stop the veg sticking to the bottom of the pan and burning.

6. Add the liquid ingredients and flavour agents. If you're making the sesame and ginger satay, first blend all the liquid ingredients together before adding them to the pan. Bring to the boil, then reduce to a simmer and cook for 10 to 15 minutes (or longer if you would like a thicker sauce).

7. Add the cooked noodles to the pan and cook for a few more minutes to allow them to absorb the flavours.

8. Taste and adjust the seasoning with more salt, pepper, acid and/ or heat if required. Use tongs to divide the noodles between four shallow bowls, then use a ladle for the sauce and veg. Garnish and serve straight away.

RECIPE:	THAI COCONUT, VEG AND NOODLE CURRY	JAPANESE UMAMI MISO RAMEN	SESAME AND GINGER SATAY	GINGER, LIME AND OYSTER MUSHROOM NOODLES
NOODLES	200g wholewheat noodles or noodles of choice	200g brown rice noodles	200g noodles of choice	200g noodles of choice
BASE VEG	5 spring onions 2 garlic cloves 1 stick of lemongrass ½ a fresh chilli ½ × thumb-size piece of fresh ginger 1 tbsp oil	5 spring onions 3 garlic cloves ½ fresh chilli ½ × thumb-size piece of fresh ginger 1 tbsp oil	2 medium onions 2 garlic cloves ½ fresh chilli ½ × thumb-size piece of fresh ginger 1 tbsp oil	5 spring onions 2 garlic cloves 1 fresh red chilli 1 × thumb-size piece of fresh ginger 1 tbsp oil
CORE INGREDIENTS	1 red pepper 1 yellow pepper ½ courgette	1 carrot 1 red pepper 150g shiitake mushrooms 50g baby spinach	300g tofu or tempeh 100g baby spinach 1 carrot, grated	250g oyster mushrooms 150g red peppers 1 courgette
SPICES	1 tbsp curry powder 1 tsp ground cumin 1 tsp ground coriander	1 tbsp paprika Pinch of chilli powder	1 tsp ground cumin 1 tsp ground coriander ½ tsp ground cinnamon	1 tsp ground cumin 1 tsp ground coriander ½ tsp ground turmeric ½ tsp ground cardamom

RECIPES AND BREAKDOWN CONTINUE ON OPPOSITE PAGE

BREAKDOWN ↑ ↓

BREAKDOWN CONTINUED	RECIPE: *CONTINUED*	THAI COCONUT, VEG AND NOODLE CURRY	JAPANESE UMAMI MISO RAMEN	SESAME AND GINGER SATAY	GINGER, LIME AND OYSTER MUSHROOM NOODLES
	LIQUID	1 × 400ml tin of coconut milk 400ml veg stock	800ml veg stock	800ml veg stock 3 tbsp almond butter 1½ tbsp apple cider vinegar 1 tbsp maple syrup	1 × 400g tin of chopped tomatoes 1 × 400ml tin of coconut milk
	FLAVOUR AGENTS	Juice of 1 lime 2½ tbsp tamari or soy sauce 1 tbsp maple syrup	Juice of 1 lemon 1 tbsp miso 1 tbsp tamari or soy sauce 1 tbsp maple syrup	Juice of 1 lime 2 tbsp tamari or soy sauce	Juice of 2 limes 2 tbsp tamari or soy sauce 1 tbsp maple syrup
	SEASONING (TO TASTE)	Salt and freshly ground black pepper Chilli flakes	Salt and freshly ground black pepper	Salt and freshly ground black pepper Chilli flakes	Salt and freshly ground black pepper Chilli flakes
	GARNISH	100g sugar snap peas Fresh coriander leaves Gomashio (p. 310)	2 spring onions, thinly sliced 1 fresh red chilli, deseeded and thinly sliced	2 tbsp sesame oil 4 tbsp gomashio (p. 310) Chopped fresh herb of choice	Flaked almonds Fresh coriander leaves

EASY ONE-POT RICE DISHES

Serves 4

Although one of the keys to making proper risotto is to cook the rice in small amounts of water that you keep replenishing so that the rice is steamed to really release its starch and sweetness, we simply boil it and it works just fine.

1. Peel and finely chop the base veg, including deseeding the chilli (if using). Peel and chop the core veg into bite-size pieces. Drain and rinse the beans (if using) and set aside.

2. Heat the oil in a large saucepan on a high heat. Add the base veg, then reduce the heat to medium and cook for 2 to 3 minutes, stirring regularly, until the onions start to brown.

3. Add the core veg, flavour agents and seasoning to the pan and cook, stirring occasionally, for a further 3 minutes.

4. Add the rice or dried lentils, stirring to coat, and cook for 1 minute.

5. Add the liquid ingredients and bring to the boil, then reduce the heat. Cover the pan with a lid and simmer for 25 minutes, until the rice and lentils (if using) are cooked and all the liquid has been absorbed. Give the rice a stir every now and again to encourage it to release its starches and become stickier. Add more stock if the rice isn't tender enough and needs further cooking. If you're making the kedgeree, be sure to stir regularly, otherwise the lentils will stick to the bottom of your pot.

6. If you're making the Indian biryani or kedgeree, stir in the beans or extras and cook for a couple of minutes more to heat them through.

7. Taste and adjust the seasoning with more salt, pepper, acid or chilli flakes if required.

8. Divide between four shallow bowls, garnish and serve. If making the Indian biryani, stir in the spinach before dividing between the bowls to allow it to wilt in the heat first.

$\rightarrow$

RECIPE:	MUSHROOM RISOTTO	INDIAN BIRYANI	KEDGEREE
BASE VEG	1 onion 2 garlic cloves 2 bay leaves 1 tbsp oil	2 onions 3 garlic cloves 1 fresh red chilli 1 × thumb-size piece of fresh ginger 1 tbsp oil	2 onions 3 garlic cloves 1 × thumb-size piece of fresh ginger 1 tbsp oil
CORE VEG	200g mushrooms (ideally oyster) 200g frozen peas, thawed	500g potatoes	1 × 400g tin of chopped tomatoes
BEANS		1 × 400g tin chickpeas 1 × 400g tin lentils 1 × 400g tin butter beans	
FLAVOUR AGENTS	2 tbsp tamari or soy sauce 1 tbsp dried mushroom powder (optional) 2 tbsp nutritional yeast 4 sprigs fresh thyme	1 tbsp curry powder 1 tsp garam masala 1 tsp cardamom 1 tsp allspice ½ tsp ground cinnamon	2 tsp garam masala 1 tsp ground turmeric 1 tsp curry powder Pinch of ground cloves
SEASONING (TO TASTE)	Salt and freshly ground black pepper Chilli flakes	Salt and freshly ground black pepper Chilli flakes	Salt and freshly ground black pepper Chilli flakes
RICE OR DRIED LENTILS	500g Arborio rice	500g short-grain brown rice	300g short-grain brown rice 200g split red lentils
LIQUID	1 litre veg stock	1.5 litres veg stock 1 × 400ml tin of coconut milk	1.4 litres veg stock
GARNISH	Lemon wedges Chilli flakes Fresh thyme leaves	100g baby spinach	Fresh coriander Sliced avocado 100g baby spinach

BREAKDOWN ↑ ↓

TOP FIVE TIPS TO ADD MORE FLAVOUR TO YOUR STEWS, CURRIES, NOODLES AND ONE-POT WONDERS

1. Layer on flavours

Your base dinner is a backdrop that you can add more flavours to, so consider adding another sauce, pickle, chutney or raita to it. We don't mean you should make a whole other sauce, but rather use the mango chutney, pickled onions, sauerkraut or kimchi that you might have in the fridge, or the jars of gomashio, dukkah or za'atar (see p. 310) that are stashed in the pantry.

Aim to add something that will contrast with the main dish to help accentuate the base flavours and widen your spectrum of flavour. For example, a pickle can be quite acidic, which creates a contrast with something that's sweet or savoury. Or stir some chopped fresh mint and lemon zest through a coconut yoghurt, to make a quick raita that will add some sharpness to complement and accentuate the sweet notes of a curry and offer a creamy, soothing softness to contrast with a spicy curry.

2. Add extra components

We tend to think of dinner in terms of one quick dish, but by adding one or two extra elements, the dinner can seem much fancier and more impressive and will have more flavour and texture. For example, you could bake some cauliflower, sweet potatoes or vegan sausages, grill some courgettes or toast some pitta breads to serve alongside, or toast some seeds or nuts to sprinkle on the top. It only takes a few small details to turn a good dinner into a great one.

3. Add more texture

Contrast is one of the keys here. Stews, curries and one-pot dishes tend to be soft and saucy, so adding something crunchy or chewy will give more contrast against those soft textures. Here are some examples of how to add more texture:

- Serve with toasted nuts or seeds (see p. 301) for crunch.

- Slice some tempeh and bake with the Asian garlic and ginger flavour bomb dressing on p. 96 to add something chewy.

- Toast some dried coconut flakes and sprinkle on top, or even make the coconut vegan bacon on p. 61.

- Toast some bread, pitta breads or roti to serve alongside, or serve with crackers.

- Serve with diced ripe avocado or guacamole to add a creamy texture.

- Make a quick salad of diced cucumber, red onion, tomato and fresh mint to serve alongside to provide a nice bite and freshness.

4. Toast your whole spices and grind them yourself

Toasting whole seeds or spices on a hot dry pan for 5 to 8 minutes, shaking the pan occasionally, will make them pop open and unlock more flavours and toasted notes. Most seeds, barks, roots and other hard or solid spices can be toasted. We normally toast any whole spices that we're using, such as cumin seeds, coriander seeds, fennel seeds, mustard seeds, peppercorns, poppy seeds, cardamom pods and whole cloves, even cinnamon sticks. Most spices that are the same size will toast in the same amount of time. Exceptions are cloves and sesame seeds, which toast more quickly due to their higher oil content.

5. Up the umami

Dave could literally drink tamari straight. We joke that one day he'll find a tamari factory that he can visit and will bring his togs in the hope that he can go for a swim in one of the tanks! All joking aside, the reason why Dave loves tamari so much is that it makes food sing. It brings another dimension of flavour by adding a sodium hit along with some umami magic.

There are many sources of umami, such as tamari, soy sauce, shoyu and miso, so try adding a little to your dish just before serving. We know that tamari and soy sauce aren't traditionally used in curries, but these condiments take a long time to ferment, so they give you a deep concentrated source of flavour and help save time when trying to add complexity and depth. Just be aware that these all contain sodium or salt, so use them carefully in conjunction with salt, as both will affect the overall salty taste of your dish.

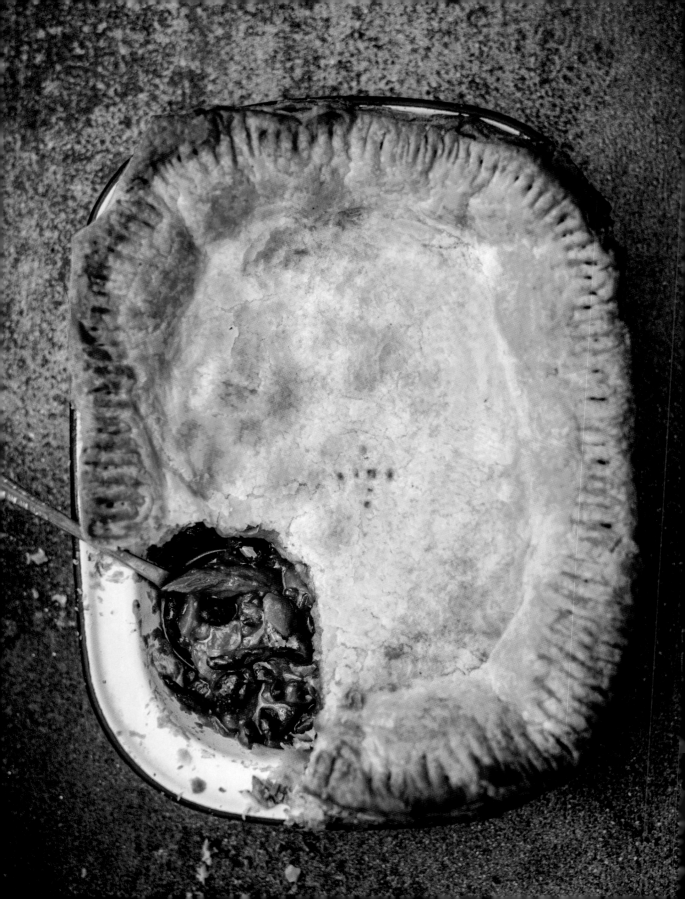

Bakes, Pies and Wellingtons

All these hearty, substantial dishes are classic comfort food. They all take a little longer to prepare than most dinners, so they tend to be more celebratory. They make a great centrepiece to a meal when someone is visiting, for family gatherings or special occasions, or for no other reason than the love of good food!

So what's the difference between a bake, a pie and a Wellington?

A bake is a very broad term that we use a lot in our cafés to refer to any stewed veg or enriched sauce that has a topping and is baked in the oven. Some of the best-known examples of a bake are a 'shepherdless' pie or cottage pie (both of which are actually bakes, not pies, despite their names – confusing, we know!). We've divided our bake recipe frameworks into two sub-categories: bakes with a mashed potato topping and bakes with other toppings, such as herbed breadcrumbs, a creamy cashew sauce (see p. 177) or an oat, nut and seed crumble.

A pie, technically speaking, needs to have a full outer layer of pastry. In the UK a petition was started to legally define what a pie is after someone tried to pass off a casserole with pastry on top as a pie. The petition only got a thousand signatures, but it shows how serious some people are about their pies!

A Wellington was originally made with beef, but our framework for vegan versions shows how versatile this dish is. A Wellington is completely encased in pastry, but the filling is a lot firmer than a pie, which means it can be sliced. A Wellington served with gravy and all the trimmings is a fantastic dish for Christmastime or any feast!

THE ESSENTIALS

The basic principles for developing each of these three dishes are the same. We usually break the filling down into four essential parts.

Base veg: You want to impart as much flavour as you can into the filling, which starts with the base. The base is almost always based around onions and garlic or some other combination of alliums, such as shallots, pearl onions or leeks (we use the white and green parts of the leek). You could also use fresh ginger or chilli if you'd like a spicy, warming note in your dish.

Core veg and beans/grains: The veg and the beans or grains are the main component of the dish, so these have a large part to play.

- **Veg:** Bakes and pies aren't fast-cooking dinners, so as a result we use starchier root veg that usually take a little longer to cook, such as regular and sweet potatoes, carrots, celeriac, parsnips and squash (just make sure to peel the squash, as the skin can be bitter, and remove the seeds). One of the veg we most enjoy in a bake, pie or Wellington is leeks. When cooked properly, leeks walk the line beautifully between sweet and savoury and are so succulent and satisfying.

- **Mushrooms:** We also love mushrooms, particularly oyster mushrooms. A trick to add more meaty texture to your bake, pie or Wellington is to cook the oyster mushrooms in a frying pan, then, using another slightly smaller pan with a clean base, press down on the mushrooms and leave them to cook for 5 to 6 minutes, without stirring, with the smaller pan on top. Turn the mushrooms over and repeat, then season with tamari or soy sauce and you have some seriously meaty mushrooms! The weight of the pan on top encourages more of the surface area of the mushrooms to brown, and encourages more water to evaporate so the mushrooms have more flavour.

- **Beans:** Beans aren't strictly essential, but they are great at bulking out the dish and adding more bite and body (not to mention more nutrition). We tend to add similar quantities of veg and beans to a bake or pie (i.e. equal parts veg to beans). We typically use tinned beans when we cook at home, because of their ease and convenience, but you can of course cook dried beans from scratch instead (see p. 302). If you do use beans, tinned or cooked chickpeas, butter beans, kidney beans, cannellini beans and lentils all work great – just be sure to drain and rinse tinned beans well before using them.

- **Grains:** For Wellingtons, we usually use cooked grains instead of beans as a major part of the filling. The cooked grains function as the starch or binder to help hold the filling together so that it doesn't fall apart when you slice it. We generally use cooked quinoa, wholemeal couscous, brown rice or breadcrumbs, but you could use bulghur wheat or pot barley too.

Sauce: The sauce has a massive impact on the flavour of your dish. The sauce or stewing liquid will reduce during the cooking and thicken from the starch in the veg and the beans or grains, making it all come together seamlessly. The sauce can include:

- Veg stock: Try our homemade version on p. 303.

- Bean broth: This is the water from cooking your own dried beans from scratch (see p. 302).

- Gravy: Add some gravy to veg stock and thicken it with a roux for a super hearty pie, such as a steak and kidney pie. See p. 262 for a few gravy variations.

- Wine: If your pie has a French theme, wine and thyme work very well. Just remember that a little goes a long way.

- Tinned tomatoes: These will add colour and a tomato undertone to the dish.

- Béchamel: This classic French white sauce can be made vegan quite easily. See our recipes for a classic béchamel and a cheesy garlic and basil version on p. 176, both of which work really well.

- Creamy cashew sauce: A creamy sauce is a tasty version of a classic béchamel, but adding cashews makes it rich and very moreish. Try any of the versions on p. 178.

- Nut butter/seed butter emulsion with water and spices: The butter emulsifies with the water to create a creamy sauce. We often season it with some base veg, such as ginger and garlic, to give the sauce a greater sense of depth.

Flavour agents: We use the same flavour agents and seasoning in these dishes that we use in all our cooking – see the list of our favourites on pp. 11–14. Just remember that the most important thing when seasoning and playing with the flavour agents is your own palate. Taste, taste and taste again, and season your dish all the way through the cooking process so that it needs only minor tweaks, if any, at the end.

BAKES

To start we have chosen three bakes that use different sauces and toppings to show you the delicious directions in which you can take your bakes. The toppings used are herby breadcrumbs, pastry and a crumble made of oats, nuts and seeds. On p. 244 there's another approach to bakes – using comforting mashed potato (regular, sweet, or a combination) as a topping.

The basic template for this framework is:

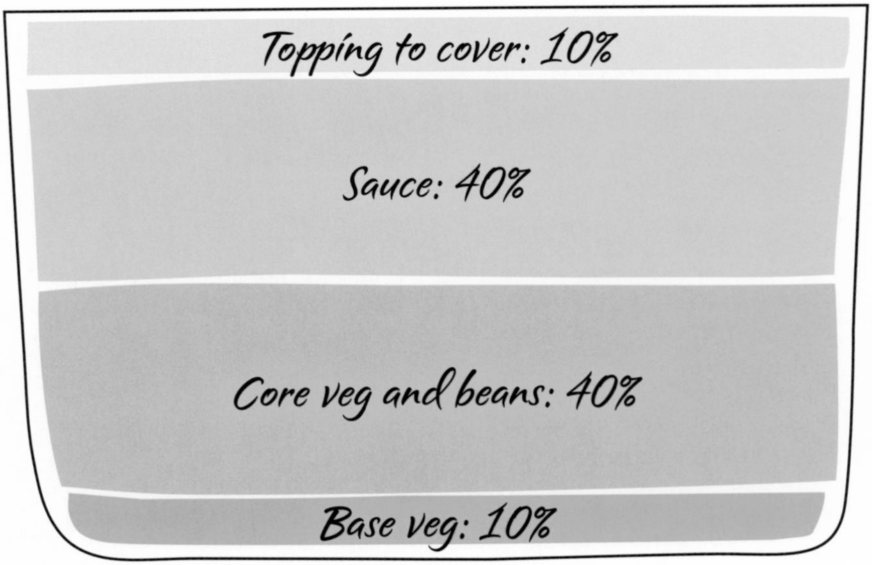

Topping to cover: 10%

Sauce: 40%

Core veg and beans: 40%

Base veg: 10%

Serves 4

1. Preheat the oven to 180°C fan/400°F/gas 6.

2. Peel and finely dice the base veg. Deseed the chilli (if using) if you want to dial down the heat. Chop the core veg into bite-size pieces. Drain and rinse the tinned beans/lentils.

3. Heat the tablespoon of oil in a large saucepan on a medium heat. Add the base veg and cook for 4 minutes, stirring regularly, until they start to brown.

4. Add the core veg and the beans along with a generous pinch of salt and some freshly ground black pepper. Stir well, put the lid on and leave to sweat for 10 to 15 minutes, stirring occasionally, until the veg are soft.

5. To deglaze the pan after cooking your veg, add a few tablespoons of water or stock to the pan. When the liquid begins to bubble, it will release all the brown bits from the bottom of the pan. One of the keys to good cooking is to never waste flavour and these brown bits have lots of it, which will add more depth to your dish, so using a wooden spoon, scrape the brown bits off the bottom of the pan and incorporate them into the veg.

6. Meanwhile, make your sauce.

   - **Creamy leek and potato pie:** Follow the instructions for making the béchamel sauce on p. 175.

   - **Mushroom and bean stroganoff pie:** Put all the ingredients in a blender or food processor and blend until super smooth.

   - **Hawaiian pie:** Put all the ingredients in a saucepan and bring to the boil, then reduce the heat and simmer for 8 minutes to allow the flavours to come together.

7. Once the veg is cooked, add the sauce and the seasoning. Bring to the boil, then reduce the heat and simmer for 10 minutes, until the sauce thickens. Taste and adjust the seasoning if needed.

8. Transfer the veg and sauce mixture to a large baking dish (approx. 32cm × 24cm), then add the topping.

   - **Creamy leek and potato pie:** Put the toast into a blender or food processor and blitz it up into breadcrumbs. Add the oil, herbs and a pinch of salt and mix well. Scatter on top of the veg and sauce mixture in a thin layer – if the layer of breadcrumbs is too thick, they will steam and end up soggy rather than crisp.

   - **Mushroom and bean stroganoff pie:** Put the oats, almonds, pumpkin seeds and cheese into a bowl and stir to combine, then stir in the oil and seasoning, making sure the oats, nuts and seeds are coated with the oil. Sprinkle over the top of the veg and sauce mixture in an even layer and not too thickly.

   - **Hawaiian pie:** Make sure the filling is cool before covering it with the pastry – this will stop the pastry going soggy. Unwrap the pastry and roll it out a bit more if needed to cover the top of your dish. Drape the rolled pastry over the top of the dish and crimp at the edges to make sure it's attached to the dish. Brush the top of the pastry with a little oat milk to help it turn golden.

9. Bake in the preheated oven for 10 to 15 minutes, until the topping is nice and golden. If you're making the Hawaiian pie, the shortcrust pastry will take a little longer to cook because the filling is cool (it will take an extra 10 minutes until the pastry is golden all over, so 20 to 25 minutes in total).

10. Remove from the oven and scatter over the garnish, then bring the dish straight to the table to allow everyone to help themselves.

RECIPE:	CREAMY LEEK AND POTATO PIE	MUSHROOM AND BEAN STROGANOFF PIE	HAWAIIAN PIE WITH PASTRY TOPPING
BASE VEG	2 medium leeks 3 garlic cloves 1 tbsp oil	2 red onions 2 garlic cloves 1 tbsp oil	2 onions 2 garlic cloves 1 x thumb-size piece of fresh ginger 1 small fresh chilli 1 tbsp oil
CORE VEG	500g potatoes	300g oyster mushrooms 300g sweet potatoes	2 yellow peppers 1 red pepper 1 sweet potato
BEANS	1 × 400g tin of butter beans	1 × 400g tin of borlotti beans	1 × 400g tin of black beans
SAUCE	700ml oat milk 1 tsp onion powder 1 tsp garlic powder Salt and freshly ground black pepper 1 bay leaf 4 tbsp oil 4 tbsp plain white flour	Juice of ½ a lemon 650ml oat milk 150g cashews 1 tbsp Dijon mustard 1 tbsp tamari or soy sauce 1 tsp garlic powder 1 tsp salt	1 × 400g tin of chopped tomatoes 300ml veg stock 100ml red wine 1 bay leaf 1 tsp garlic powder 1 tsp salt

BREAKDOWN ↑ ↓

RECIPES AND BREAKDOWN CONTINUE ON OPPOSITE PAGE

RECIPE: *CONTINUED*	CREAMY LEEK AND POTATO PIE	MUSHROOM AND BEAN STROGANOFF PIE	HAWAIIAN PIE WITH PASTRY TOPPING
SEASONING	Juice of ½ a lemon 3 sprigs of fresh thyme, leaves stripped from the stalks Salt and freshly ground black pepper (to taste)	Salt and freshly ground black pepper (to taste)	2 tbsp tamari or soy sauce 2 tbsp maple syrup 1 tsp smoked paprika
TOPPING	4 slices of brown bread, toasted 2 tbsp oil 1 tbsp dried oregano Pinch of salt	100g oats 50g flaked almonds 50g pumpkin seeds 50g grated vegan cheese 2 tbsp oil Salt and freshly ground black pepper	1 sheet of shop-bought vegan shortcrust pastry, thawed 2 tbsp oat milk
GARNISH	Chopped fresh flat-leaf parsley	Chopped fresh flat-leaf parsley	½ pineapple, peeled, cored and diced

BREAKDOWN *CONTINUED*

BAKES WITH A MASHED POTATO TOPPING

Our recipe framework on pp. 248–9 includes three variations so that you get an idea of your options, but the essentials of this framework are:

Potatoes: 40%

Sauce: 20%

Core veg and beans: 30%

Base veg: 10%

→

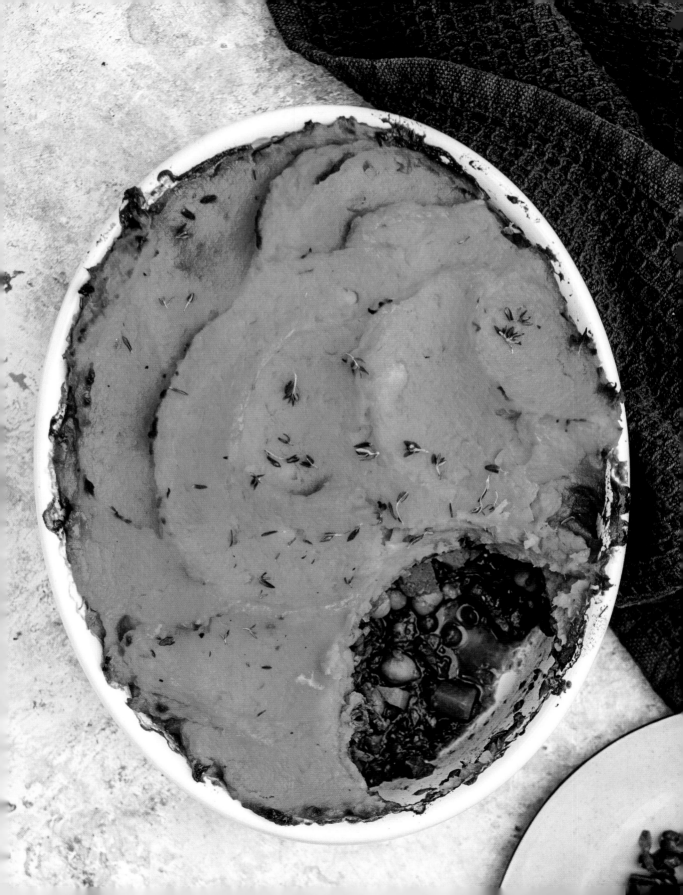

Serves 6

1. Preheat the oven to 200°C fan/425°F/gas 7.

2. Peel and finely dice the base veg. Deseed the chilli (if using) if you want to dial down the heat. Peel the core veg and chop into bite-size pieces. Drain and rinse the tinned beans/lentils.

3. Heat the tablespoon of oil in a large saucepan on a medium heat. Add the base veg and cook for 4 to 6 minutes, stirring regularly, until they start to brown.

4. Add the core veg and the beans/lentils along with a generous pinch of salt and some freshly ground black pepper. Stir well, put the lid on and leave to sweat for 10 to 15 minutes, stirring occasionally, until the veg are soft.

5. To deglaze the pan after cooking your veg, add a few tablespoons of water or stock to the pan. When the liquid begins to bubble, it will release all the brown bits from the bottom of the pan. One of the keys to good cooking is to never waste flavour and these brown bits have lots of it, which will add more depth to your dish, so, using a wooden spoon, scrape the brown bits off the bottom of the pan and incorporate them into the veg.

6. Once the veg are cooked, add the sauce ingredients and the seasoning. If making the fishless pie, add the wine first and bring to the boil to allow the alcohol to evaporate before adding the cashew cream and veg stock. Bring to the boil, then reduce the heat and simmer for 10 minutes, until the sauce thickens. Taste and adjust the seasoning if needed.

7. Meanwhile, to make the mashed potato topping, cut the potatoes and/or sweet potatoes into bite-size pieces. (We like to leave the skin on our potatoes since that's where a lot of nutrition is and to give our bakes a more rustic look.) Put the potatoes and/or sweet potatoes into a large saucepan of cold salted water. Bring to the boil, then reduce the heat and cook for 10 to 15 minutes, until tender. Drain the potatoes, then return them to the hot saucepan for a few minutes to let them dry out. Add the oat milk and olive oil, then mash until smooth. Season well with salt and pepper.

8. Transfer the veg and sauce mixture to a large baking dish (approx. 32cm x 24cm), then add the mashed potatoes on top. The dish should be two-thirds full with the veg and sauce mixture and the remaining one-third should be the mashed potato topping. Use the tines of a fork to make drills on the mash, which will turn crisp and golden in the oven.

9. Bake in the preheated oven for 15 minutes, until the potato topping starts to turn golden and the sauce is bubbling.

10. To serve, garnish with a few sprigs of fresh thyme or serve with some pesto on the side, then bring the dish straight to the table to allow everyone to help themselves.

RECIPE:	SHEPHERDLESS PIE	SWEET POTATO COTTAGE PIE	FISHLESS PIE
BASE VEG	2 onions 3 garlic cloves 1 tbsp oil	1 medium leek 2 garlic cloves 1 tbsp oil	1 red onion 3 garlic cloves 1 small fresh red chilli
CORE VEG	1 carrot 1 parsnip 10 fine beans A few sprigs of fresh flat-leaf parsley	100g green beans 1 carrot 1 parsnip	100g oyster mushrooms 3 potatoes 1 carrot 1 leek ½ a celeriac
BEANS/LENTILS	2 × 400g tins of lentils	1 × 400g tin of lentils 1 × 400g tin of chickpeas	1 × 400g tin of black beans
SAUCE	2 × 400g tins of chopped tomatoes	800ml veg stock	100ml white wine 350g cashew cream sauce (p. 177) 450ml veg stock

RECIPES AND BREAKDOWN CONTINUE ON OPPOSITE PAGE

RECIPE: *CONTINUED*	SHEPHERDLESS PIE	SWEET POTATO COTTAGE PIE	FISHLESS PIE
SEASONING	2 bay leaves 2 tbsp tamari or soy sauce 1 tbsp maple syrup 1 tsp smoked paprika 1 tsp salt ½ tsp ground black pepper (to taste)	6 sprigs of fresh thyme, leaves stripped 3 tbsp tamari or soy sauce ½ tsp chilli powder Salt and freshly ground black pepper (to taste)	100g samphire (or add 1 extra tbsp of dulse and some leafy green veg such as spinach) 6 sprigs of fresh thyme, leaves stripped 1 tbsp milled dulse seaweed 1 tsp salt ¼ tsp ground black pepper
MASHED POTATO TOPPING	1.5kg potatoes, skin on 100ml oat milk 3 tbsp olive oil Salt and freshly ground black pepper (to taste)	750g potatoes 750g sweet potatoes 100ml oat milk 3 tbsp olive oil Salt and freshly ground black pepper (to taste)	1.5kg potatoes, skin on 100ml oat milk 3 tbsp olive oil Salt and freshly ground black pepper (to taste)
TO SERVE	A few sprigs of fresh thyme	Coriander pesto (p. 167)	Any pesto from p. 167

BREAKDOWN *CONTINUED*

PIES

Serves 4 to 6

Each pie in the framework is made with a different sauce, but you can easily mix and match to make your own variations. Each pie is made using 800g of veg and beans in total to 800ml of sauce, so the filling is nice and thick when baked in the pastry. Our favourite pastry for pies is puff pastry, but you could use filo or shortcrust pastry if you prefer.

1. Thaw your pastry overnight in the fridge.

2. Preheat the oven to 200°C fan/425°F/gas 7.

3. Peel and finely dice the base veg. Deseed the chilli (if using) if you want to dial down the heat. Peel the core veg and chop into bite-size pieces. Drain and rinse the tinned beans.

4. You will have to blind bake the pastry to seal it, which means the pastry will be able to take a moist sauce and still be cooked through. To blind bake the pastry, grease a pie dish with 1 tablespoon of oil. Roll out one sheet of pastry to fit the pie dish, ensuring the pastry comes up and slightly over the edges, as it will shrink a little when it bakes. Cover with parchment paper and weigh it down with about 200g of dried beans. Bake in the preheated oven for 15 minutes, then remove the parchment paper and dried beans and leave the pastry to cool on a wire rack while you make the filling.

5. Heat the tablespoon of oil in a large saucepan on a medium heat. Add the base veg and cook for 4 minutes, stirring regularly, until they start to brown. Add the spices (if using) and cook for 30 seconds, stirring continuously.

6. Add the core veg and the beans/lentils (if using) along with a generous pinch of salt and some freshly ground black pepper. Stir well, put the lid on and leave to sweat for 10 to 15 minutes, stirring occasionally, until the veg are soft.

7. To deglaze the pan after cooking your veg, add a few tablespoons of water or stock to the pan. When the liquid begins to bubble, it will release all the brown bits from the bottom of the pan. One of the keys to good cooking is to never waste flavour and these brown bits have lots of it, which will add more depth to your dish, so, using a wooden spoon, scrape the brown bits off the bottom of the pan and incorporate them into the veg.

8. Meanwhile, make the sauce.

9. Steak and kidney pie: Make a roux by heating the oil in a small saucepan on a medium heat, then sift in the flour and whisk for 1 minute. Stir in the stock. Bring to the boil, then reduce the heat and simmer for 5 to 8 minutes, stirring continuously, until thickened, then take the pan off the heat.

10. Creamy broccoli pie: Follow the instructions for making the béchamel sauce on p. 175.

11. Once the veg is cooked, add the sauce and seasoning. Bring to the boil, then reduce the heat and simmer for 10 to 15 minutes, until the sauce thickens. Taste and adjust the seasoning if needed.

12. Add the veg and sauce mixture to the blind baked pie base until it comes to almost the top. Roll out the remaining sheet of pastry to fit the top of the pie dish, then gently place it on top. Use the tines of a fork to press the two sheets of pastry together and to seal the pie, then trim off any excess pastry. Make a hole in the middle of the pastry using the tines of a fork to allow the steam and extra moisture to escape. Using a pastry brush, brush the non-dairy milk on top of the pastry to help it turn golden.

13. Bake the pie in the preheated oven for 15 to 20 minutes, until the pastry is nice and golden and the sauce is bubbling.

RECIPE:	STEAK AND KIDNEY PIE	CREAMY BROCCOLI PIE	CHOCOLATE CHILLI PIE
PASTRY	1 tbsp oil 2 sheets of puff pastry 2 tbsp non-dairy milk	1 tbsp oil 2 sheets of puff pastry 2 tbsp non-dairy milk	1 tbsp oil 2 sheets of puff pastry 2 tbsp non-dairy milk
BASE VEG	2 onions 4 garlic cloves 1 tbsp oil	2 medium leeks 1 tbsp oil	1 red onion 3 garlic cloves 1 small fresh chilli 1 tbsp oil
SPICES	1 tsp garlic powder ½ tsp smoked paprika		1 tbsp ground cumin 1 tbsp ground coriander 1 tsp salt ½ tsp smoked paprika
CORE VEG	1 carrot 400g mushrooms (ideally oyster mushrooms)	400g broccoli 400g celeriac, potato or parsnip	1 red pepper 1 yellow pepper 1 aubergine

← BREAKDOWN →

RECIPES AND BREAKDOWN CONTINUE ON OPPOSITE PAGE

RECISE: *CONTINUED*	STEAK AND KIDNEY PIE	CREAMY BROCCOLI PIE	CHOCOLATE CHILLI PIE
BEANS	1 × 400g tin of kidney beans		1 × 400g tin of kidney beans
SAUCE	6 tbsp oil 6 tbsp plain white flour 800ml veg stock	700ml oat milk 1 tsp onion powder 1 tsp garlic powder Salt and freshly ground black pepper 1 bay leaf 4 tbsp oil 4 tbsp plain white flour	2 × 400g tins of chopped tomatoes
SEASONING	4 sprigs of fresh thyme, leaves stripped 2 bay leaves 4 tbsp tamari or soy sauce Salt and freshly ground black pepper (to taste)	Zest and juice of ½ a lemon 1 tbsp Dijon mustard	Juice of ½ a lime 65g dark chocolate, finely chopped

← **BREAKDOWN** *CONTINUED* →

WELLINGTONS

A few years ago we had a chestnut and cashew Wellington as the centrepiece for our first fully vegan Christmas. We had 17 family members over for dinner and it went down a treat – even our aunt, uncle and cousins adored it. We've made a vegan Wellington for Christmas dinner ever since, complete with gravy (p. 261), cranberry sauce and a couple of sides.

The most famous incarnation of this traditional British dish is a beef Wellington. We've made many types of Wellingtons over the years and define it as some sort of reasonably solid filling wrapped in puff pastry and baked in the oven that can be sliced.

The following is a breakdown of one Wellington, which will serve four to six people (the recipes in our framework make two Wellingtons). As with pies, our favourite pastry to use is puff pastry, but feel free to use filo or shortcrust pastry if you prefer.

Puff pastry: 15%

Flavour agents and seasoning: 10%

Starchy cooked grain: 15%

Nuts/seeds: 15%

Core veg: 30%

Base veg: 15%

Makes 2 Wellingtons

1. Thaw your pastry overnight in the fridge.

2. Preheat the oven to 180°C fan/400°F/gas 6. Line two baking trays with non-stick baking paper.

3. Peel and finely chop your base veg (if you're making the beet Wellington, use the white and green parts of the leek). Chop any rough gnarly bits off your core veg, then grate them (no need to peel, as a lot of the goodness is in the skin). Drain the tinned jackfruit and chop into bite-size pieces (if using). Cut the oyster mushrooms into small strips (if using).

4. To toast the nuts, put them in a hot, dry frying pan on a high heat and toast for 5 to 8 minutes, stirring occasionally, until they start to turn golden, making sure they don't burn. Tip out on to a plate and set aside to cool.

5. Heat the oil in a large frying pan or saucepan on a medium heat. Add the base veg and cook for 5 minutes, stirring regularly, until they start to turn translucent and golden.

6. Add the core veg along with a generous pinch of salt and some freshly ground black pepper. Stir well, put the lid on and leave to sweat for 10 minutes, stirring occasionally, until the veg are soft.

7. To deglaze the pan after cooking your veg, add a few tablespoons of water or stock to the pan. When the liquid begins to bubble, it will release all the brown bits from the bottom of the pan. One of the keys to good cooking is to never waste flavour and these brown bits have lots of it, which will add more depth to your dish, so, using a wooden spoon, scrape the brown bits off the bottom of the pan and incorporate them into the veg. Remove the pan from the heat.

8. Crush two-thirds of the toasted nuts by putting them in a food processor and pulsing until they are finely chopped. If you don't have a food processor, you can crush them by wrapping them in a clean tea towel and bashing them with a small pan or rolling pin. Add the chopped and whole nuts to the pan.

9. Strip the leaves of the fresh herbs from their stalks and roughly chop, discarding the stalks. Add to the pan along with the remaining flavour agents and seasoning. Taste the filling and adjust the seasoning if you think it needs any more salt or pepper.

10. Add the cooked grain/starch to the filling and put the pan back on a medium heat. Cook for a couple of minutes, stirring, until everything is warm and well mixed. Remove from the heat again, then taste and adjust the seasoning one last time if needed.

11. To assemble the Wellingtons, roll out each sheet of thawed puff pastry. Divide the filling in half, then spoon the filling into the centre of each sheet of pastry, leaving one-third of the pastry clear on either side and also leaving a little space clear on each end so that you can properly seal the Wellington. Form the filling into a smooth mound, then gather up the pastry so that it completely encloses and overlaps the filling. Seal the pastry at both ends as you would a parcel, trimming away any excess pastry.

12. Now it's time to invert the Wellingtons on to the lined trays so they're seam side down. Using the baking paper to help you transfer each Wellington, gently roll it over so that it's seam side down on the tray. Score the top of the pastry with the back of a knife, making sure not to cut all the way through the pastry. Using a pastry brush, brush the non-dairy milk on top of the pastry to help it turn golden.

13. Bake in the preheated oven for 25 to 30 minutes, until the pastry is golden brown and the kitchen smells fab! It may take a little longer depending on your oven, but what you're looking for is that the pastry is nice and golden.

14. Serve with gravy (p. 261) and all your favourite sides to make this a wonderful centrepiece of any special meal.

$\rightarrow$

RECIPE:	CELERIAC AND CASHEW WELLINGTON	BEET WELLINGTON WITH JACKFRUIT AND PEANUTS	SWEET POTATO, MUSHROOM AND WALNUT WELLINGTON
PASTRY	2 sheets of puff pastry 2 tbsp non-dairy milk	2 sheets of puff pastry 2 tbsp non-dairy milk	2 sheets of puff pastry 2 tbsp non-dairy milk
BASE VEG	3 small onions 3 garlic cloves 2 tbsp oil	2 leeks 2 garlic cloves 2 tbsp oil	200g shallots 3 garlic cloves 2 tbsp oil
CORE VEG	200g carrots 200g celeriac or parsnip	200g tinned jackfruit 100g carrots 100g beetroot	200g sweet potato 200g oyster mushrooms
NUTS	200g cashews	200g peanuts	200g walnuts
FLAVOUR AGENTS AND SEASONING	A few sprigs of fresh thyme 3 tbsp tamari or soy sauce 1 tsp salt ½ tsp black pepper ½ tsp chilli powder or cayenne pepper	1 sprig of fresh rosemary Juice of 1 lime 3 tbsp tamari or soy sauce 1 tsp salt ½ tsp ground black pepper	15g fresh mint Juice of ½ a lemon 3 tbsp tamari or soy sauce 1 tsp salt ½ tsp ground black pepper
GRAIN/ STARCH	200g cooked quinoa (p. 301)	200g cooked wholemeal couscous (p. 301)	200g dried breadcrumbs

← BREAKDOWN →

EASY SUPER TASTY GRAVY

Makes approx. 500ml

Gravy is such a core part of many celebratory dinners. If you're making the basic gravy, we think it's worth getting the nutritional yeast if you don't usually have it, as it's a store cupboard staple that lasts for a long time and any good health food store will stock it. We've given you three easy gravy recipes that take only 10 minutes to make: one basic one that works for everything and two variations to show how you can adapt your gravy to your palate or the dish you're serving it with.

1. Peel and finely chop the base veg. Deseed the chilli (if using) if you want to dial down the heat.

2. Heat the base veg oil in a small non-stick saucepan on a high heat. Add the base veg and cook for 3 to 5 minutes, stirring regularly, until they start to turn golden.

3. Mix together the liquid and seasoning in a large jug, then pour into the pan. Bring to the boil, then reduce the heat down to a gentle simmer.

4. Remove 5 tablespoons of the sauce to a bowl and sift in the thickener, mixing well until it's homogeneous. Add to the rest of the sauce. Stir in the oil and cook for a further 3 to 4 minutes, until the gravy has thickened. For a thicker consistency and stronger taste, let it simmer for longer. However, if it's too thick or tastes too strong, you can dilute it by whisking in a little boiling water or stock to reach your desired taste and consistency.

5. Place a fine mesh sieve over a 1 litre jug or a large bowl, then pour the gravy through the sieve and into the jug or bowl to remove any lumps. Transfer to a gravy boat and serve hot.

RECIPE:	BASIC GRAVY	FRENCH SHALLOT, WINE AND THYME GRAVY	SPICY GINGER GRAVY
BASE VEG	1 onion 1½ tbsp oil	4 shallots 2 garlic cloves 1½ tbsp oil	1 onion 1 fresh red chilli ½ a thumb-size piece of fresh ginger 1½ tbsp oil
LIQUID	500ml vegetable stock 4 tbsp tamari or soy sauce	400ml vegetable stock 100ml red wine 2 tbsp tamari or soy sauce	500ml vegetable stock 4 tbsp tamari or soy sauce
SEASONING	4 tbsp nutritional yeast 2 tsp garlic powder Freshly ground black pepper (to taste)	3 sprigs of fresh thyme, leaves removed from stalks Freshly ground black pepper (to taste)	Juice of ½ a lime 1 tbsp maple syrup 1 tsp garlic powder Freshly ground black pepper (to taste)
THICKENER	3 tbsp cornflour	3 tbsp cornflour	3 tbsp cornflour
OIL	4 tbsp olive oil	4 tbsp olive oil	4 tbsp olive oil

BREAKDOWN

Sweet Stuff

Rather than trying to make 'healthier' treats using wholefood ingredients, we're going all out to try to make vegan treats that are as tasty as possible, so please forgive us if you were hoping to find black bean brownies or chickpea blondies!

THE ESSENTIALS

So how do you make brownies, cookies, cupcakes or a classic Victoria sponge, carrot cake or chocolate fudge cake that are not only vegan but taste great too? At the simplest level, baking usually involves some variation of these six essential elements.

Flour: If you want your vegan treats to look and taste like a more traditional cake or cookie, use white flour. The more brown or wholemeal flour you use, the more you are moving away from cake and towards bread! Plus, due to its higher fibre content, using wholemeal flour will mean that the flour is heavier and generally won't rise as much, resulting in a denser texture.

Sweetener: There are many arguments as to what the best or healthiest sweetener is, but in reality, a healthy sweetener doesn't exist – it's a bit like asking which doughnut is the healthiest. Whether you use caster sugar or a liquid sweetener such as maple syrup, they serve the same function. Our stance on sweetener is that less is best, but having said that, we love cake as much as the next person, so if you're having a treat, just enjoy it.

Fat: How do you replace butter, the classic fat that is used most often in baking, in vegan treats? There are many options, including using a liquid oil, such as sunflower oil, or a more saturated fat that is solid at room temperature, such as cacao butter or coconut oil.

Binders: Instead of hen's eggs we usually go with a flax or chia 'egg' (see p. 303), but sometimes we use almond butter or even bananas as a binder.

Raising agents: Baking powder is what we use most often, as it requires just heat and moisture to work. On the other hand bread soda (also known as bicarbonate of soda) needs an acid to activate its rising properties.

Flavour agents: The flavour agents will determine the type of sponge or cake you want to make. For example, using the same base recipe, you might prefer vanilla for a classic Victoria sponge cake, whereas if you add cocoa powder it will become a chocolate cake. Or if you add raisins, grated carrot and other dried fruit, it can become a carrot cake.

BROWNIES

Brownies are like a cross between a chocolate cake, fudge and a cookie. Legend has it that brownies were invented by a careless chef who forgot to put the raising agent into a chocolate cake and served it as flat cakes to be eaten by hand instead, although another story says that a chef added melted chocolate to a biscuit batter and baked it in a pan. No matter which version you choose to believe, everyone has their own ideas about what the perfect brownie is. Some people (like us!) prefer a gooey, fudgy brownie, while others love a cakey brownie.

We did more than thirty trials in search of vegan brownie nirvana, so we really got to understand what the main variables are that you can play with and how the essential ingredients interact with each other. We've also included one blondie recipe in the framework. A blondie is a brownie without chocolate, so it's blonde in colour – hence the name!

THE ESSENTIALS

The composition of a traditional brownie is based on seven essential components.

Fat: We were told numerous times by many baker friends that we could never make a decent gooey, fudgy brownie without butter, but we have proved them wrong! Butter is typically around 80–82% fat, 16–17% water, and 1–2% milk solids (and may also contain some salt, if it's salted butter), whereas oil is 100% fat. Oil is lighter than butter, which means that the texture of cakes that use oil is lighter too. The water in butter can strengthen and activate the gluten in a brownie or cake, resulting in a crumb and texture that are denser and not quite as tender as an oil-based cake. Oil-based cakes or brownies also tend to dry out less quickly compared to cakes or brownies made with butter, so if you want a brownie that stays moist and gooey, use oil rather than butter. We like to use a neutral-tasting sunflower oil. The other portion of fat comes from the cacao butter in the chocolate.

Sugar: We use coconut sugar in our brownies as it has a slightly lower glycaemic index (GI) value than golden caster sugar, which means it won't make your blood sugar levels spike quite as quickly as caster sugar. But if you can't find coconut sugar, just use an equal amount of golden caster sugar or brown sugar. The other portion of sweetener comes from the sugar in the chocolate.

Binder: A flax 'egg' functions as a binder and also gives some structure and a slight raising effect.

Flour: If you want your vegan brownies to taste as indulgent as possible, you have to use white flour.

Raising agent: We always add a small amount of baking powder, which helps the brownies to rise a little.

Flavourings: We usually use a 54% dark chocolate in our brownies, and vanilla extract. The higher the percentage of cocoa solids in the chocolate, the more bitter it is.

Non-dairy milk: We normally use rice milk in brownies, as it's naturally sweet, or unsweetened almond milk, but feel free to use whichever non-dairy milk you have on hand. The milk loosens the batter and gives it more moisture.

Makes 10 to 15

1. If making the fudgy hazelnut brownies, preheat the oven to 180°C fan/400°F/ gas 6. Spread the hazelnuts out on a baking tray, then toast in the preheated oven for 10 minutes. Remove from the oven and place in a tea towel. Rub them until the skins are removed. Roughly chop and set aside, then reduce the oven temperature to 160°C fan/350°F/gas 4.

2. For the fudgy brownies, cakey brownies or blondies, preheat the oven to 160°C fan/350°F/gas 4. For all recipes, line a 30cm × 20cm pan with baking parchment.

3. If you're making any of the brownies, roughly chop the chocolate, then place in a heatproof bowl set over a pan of gently simmering water, making sure the water doesn't touch the bottom of the bowl. Allow to gently melt, then set aside to cool slightly. If you're making the blondies, chop the chocolate into chunks.

4. Meanwhile, to make the flax 'egg', put the ground flax seeds and water into a small bowl and leave to coagulate for 5 minutes or so. The ground flax will soak up all the liquid and form a gloopy, glue-like consistency.

5. Sift the flour, baking powder and salt into a large bowl, then add the sugar and stir to combine. Add the oil (and the almond butter if making the blondies), then beat by hand with a wooden spoon or with an electric mixer. Add the melted chocolate, non-dairy milk and flavour agents and beat again for 2 to 3 minutes, until smooth. If making the blondies, stir in the chocolate chunks.

6. Simply pour the batter into the lined pan, then smooth the top.

7. Bake in the preheated oven for the required baking time:

- **Fudgy or fudgy hazelnut brownies:** 30 to 35 minutes, until a skewer inserted into the centre comes out almost clean.

- **Cakey brownies:** 30 minutes, until a skewer inserted into the centre comes out almost clean.

- **Blondies:** 50 minutes, until a skewer inserted into the centre comes out almost clean.

8. Remove from the oven and leave to cool fully on a wire rack before cutting into portions. For both fudgy brownies remove from the oven and leave to cool for 10 minutes then pop in the fridge to set for 40 minutes, for the perfect fudgy brownie. This can often be one of the hardest parts of making brownies, but it's essential if you want them to set and firm up to the correct texture.

RECIPE:	FUDGY BROWNIES	FUDGY HAZELNUT BROWNIES	CAKEY BROWNIES	ALMOND BLONDIES WITH CHOCOLATE CHUNKS
DARK CHOCOLATE (54% CACAO SOLIDS)	350g dark chocolate	350g dark chocolate	250g dark chocolate	60g dark chocolate
FLAX 'EGG'	1½ tbsp ground flax seeds 4½ tbsp water	1½ tbsp ground flax seeds 4½ tbsp water	2 tbsp ground flax seeds 6 tbsp water	2 tbsp ground flax seeds 6 tbsp water
FLOUR	200g plain white flour	200g plain white flour	300g plain white flour	300g plain white flour
BAKING POWDER	1 tsp baking powder	1 tsp baking powder	2 tsp baking powder	2 tsp baking powder
SALT	Pinch of salt	Pinch of salt	Pinch of salt	Pinch of salt
SUGAR	125g coconut, golden caster or brown sugar	125g coconut, golden caster or brown sugar	175g coconut, golden caster or brown sugar	250g coconut, golden caster or brown sugar
OIL/FAT	125ml sunflower oil	125ml sunflower oil	125ml sunflower oil	150ml sunflower oil 150g almond butter
NON-DAIRY MILK	50ml rice milk or unsweetened almond milk	50ml rice milk or unsweetened almond milk	125ml rice milk or unsweetened almond milk	175ml rice milk or unsweetened almond milk
FLAVOUR AGENTS	1 tbsp vanilla extract	100g hazelnuts 1 tbsp vanilla extract	1 tbsp vanilla extract	1 tbsp vanilla extract

BREAKDOWN ↑ ↓

CHOCOLATE CHIP COOKIES

Like brownies, everyone has their own preference for what makes the perfect chocolate chip cookie, whether it's chewy, biscuity or more like a shortbread. Being Irish, we have a serious soft spot for the humble oat and have sometimes joked that we have porridge running through our blood, so we adore the chewy oat chocolate chip cookie. When we first started the shop we got to know this wonderful lady called Joan Orr, who we later called Granny Orr – we used to bring potential girlfriends up to Joan for her to help us vet them! She always loved shortbread cookies and was forever offering them to us, so this one is for you, Granny Orr!

We have provided a framework with four different chocolate chip cookies so that you can better understand the components and the relationships between the starch, fat, sweetener and flavouring and see how if you simply increase the amount of flour in the chewy chocolate chip cookie, for example, you will end up with more of a shortbread-style cookie. If you aren't a chocolate lover, you can easily replace the chocolate chips with raisins or some other dried fruit, such as chopped apricots, or nuts, such as shelled chopped pistachios.

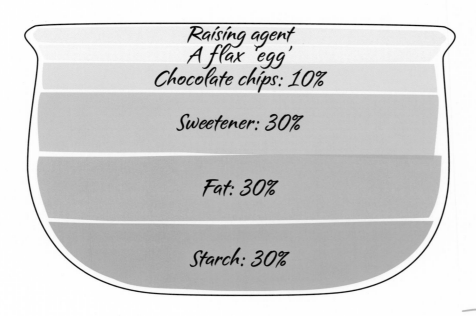

Raising agent
A flax 'egg'
Chocolate chips: 10%

Sweetener: 30%

Fat: 30%

Starch: 30%

Chewy or biscuity chocolate chip cookies:

1. To make the flax 'egg', put the ground flax seeds and water in a small bowl and leave to coagulate for 5 minutes or so.

2. Sift the flour, raising agents and salt into a large bowl, then stir in the sugar.

3. To prepare the fat, whisk together the oil and almond butter until well combined. Mix the fat mixture into the dry ingredients along with the flavour agent (the vanilla) and the flax 'egg'.

4. Using a spatula or by hand, bring the mixture together into a dough, then add 50g of the chocolate chips and mix them through the dough.

5. Line a large baking tray with non-stick baking paper. Weigh out 60g of dough for each cookie (you should get 6 cookies), then roll into a ball. Place the cookies on the lined baking tray with enough room between them for them to spread during cooking. Pat each one down flat with the palm of your hand, then add a few of the remaining chocolate chips on top of each cookie.

6. Chill the tray of cookies in the fridge for 30 minutes.

7. Preheat the oven to 150°C fan/325°F/gas 3.

8. Bake the cookies in the preheated oven for 11 minutes if making the chewy cookies or 15 to 16 minutes if making the biscuity cookies, until they start to turn golden but before they start to burn. Allow to cool on the tray for 5 minutes, then transfer to a wire rack and allow to cool fully to firm up.

Shortbread-style chocolate chip cookies:

1. Preheat the oven to 150°C fan/325°F/gas 3. Line a large baking tray with non-stick baking paper.

2. Sieve the flour and salt into a large bowl, then stir in the sugar. Note that coconut sugar will result in a darker cookie, but you can use regular caster sugar or xylitol for a more traditional-looking shortbread.

3. Add the fat (the coconut oil) to the dry ingredients, then use your fingertips to rub it in until it is fully incorporated and you get a breadcrumb-like texture. Alternatively, you can put the flour, salt, sugar and coconut oil in a food processor and pulse just until the mixture looks like breadcrumbs, taking care not to overmix.

4. Add the chocolate chips, then bring together into a dough. The dough will be loose but will pack together to form a cookie.

5. Divide the dough into 6 or 7 balls, then press down and shape into round cookies. Place on the lined baking tray.

6. Bake in the preheated oven for 25 minutes, until they start to firm up. Allow to cool on the tray for a few minutes, then transfer to a wire rack and allow to cool fully so that they firm up.

Chewy oat chocolate chip cookies:

1. Preheat the oven to 180°C fan/400°F/gas 6. Line a large baking tray with non-stick baking paper.

2. To make the flax 'egg', put the ground flax seeds and water in a small bowl and leave to coagulate for 5 minutes or so.

3. Put the starch (the oats and coconut) into a large bowl. However, if you don't like coconut, leave it out and replace it with an extra 30g of oats. Add the raising agent, salt, and sugar.

4. Put the fat (the nut butter) and flavour agents (the maple syrup and vanilla) into a bowl and mix well, until fully combined. Mix the fat mixture into the dry ingredients along with the flax 'egg' – this is easiest done by hand. Add the chocolate chips and bring together into a dough.

5. Weigh out 60g of dough for each cookie (you should get 7 cookies), then roll into a ball. Place the cookies on the lined baking tray with enough room between them for them to spread during cooking. Pat each one down flat with the palm of your hand.

6. Bake in the preheated oven for 12 to 14 minutes, until they start to turn golden but before they start to burn. Allow to cool on the tray for 5 minutes, then transfer to a wire rack and allow to cool fully.

RECIPE:	CHEWY CHOCOLATE CHIP COOKIES MAKES 6	BISCUITY CHOCOLATE CHIP COOKIES MAKES 6	SHORTBREAD-STYLE CHOCOLATE COOKIES MAKES 6 OR 7	CHEWY OAT CHOCOLATE CHIP COOKIES MAKES 7
FLAX 'EGG'	1 tbsp ground flax seeds 3 tbsp water	1 tbsp ground flax seeds 3 tbsp water		1 tbsp ground flax seeds 3 tbsp water
FLOUR / STARCH	125g plain white flour	125g plain white flour	220g plain white flour	90g rolled oats 30g desiccated coconut
RAISING AGENTS	1½ tsp baking powder ½ tsp baking soda	1½ tsp baking powder ½ tsp baking soda		1 tsp baking powder
SALT	Pinch of salt	Pinch of salt	Pinch of salt	Pinch of salt
SUGAR	110g coconut sugar	80g coconut sugar	100g coconut sugar	100g coconut sugar
FAT	60g sunflower oil 45g almond butter	60g sunflower oil 45g almond butter	110g coconut oil	125g almond or peanut butter
FLAVOUR AGENTS	½ tsp vanilla extract	½ tsp vanilla extract		2 tbsp maple syrup 1 tsp vanilla extract
CHOCOLATE CHIPS	60g dark chocolate chips	60g dark chocolate chips	60g dark chocolate chips	40g dark chocolate chips

BREAKDOWN ↑ ↓

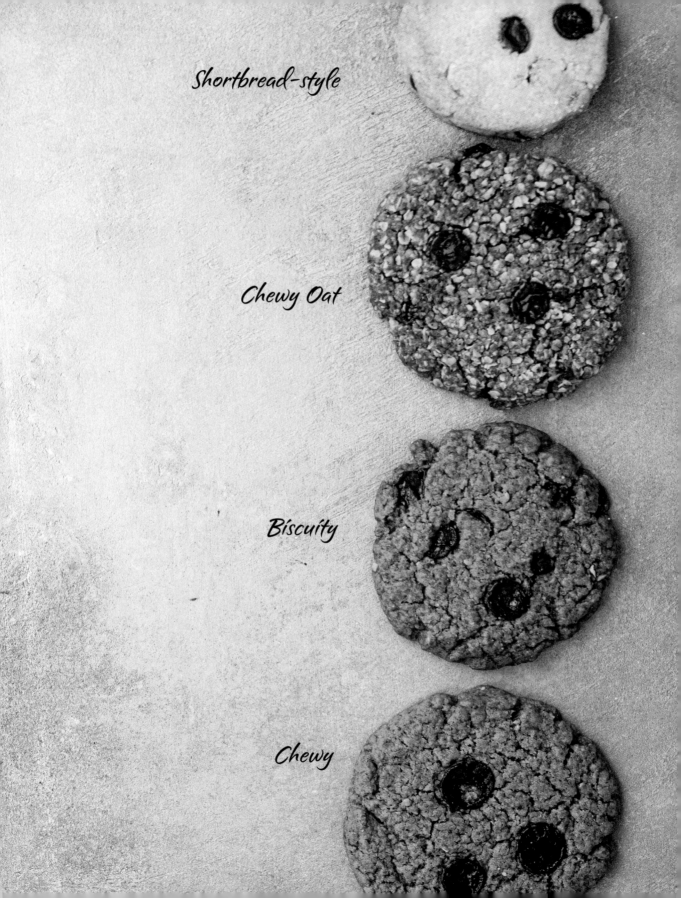

Shortbread-style

Chewy Oat

Biscuity

Chewy

CUPCAKES

Makes 12 cupcakes

When our mom used to make fairy cakes for us four boys, she'd cut a small circle out of the top of the cupcake, fill it with whipped cream, then cut the circle in two and use the halves to create wings on top – we devoured them! The recipes below are in honour of our mom and those wonderful fairy cakes. In this framework we give a base recipe for a simple vanilla cupcake and show how we make small changes to give two different types of cupcakes: red velvet and courgette and lime. The cupcakes are a little one-dimensional on their own, so to give them an extra layer of flavour and texture, top them with frosting to give them that sense of indulgence.

1. Preheat the oven to 180°C fan/400°F/gas 6. Line a 12-cup muffin tray with paper cases.

2. Sift the flour and raising agents into a large bowl, then stir in the sweetener. If you're making the vanilla cupcakes, note that the coconut sugar will give you a darker cupcake than if you use white caster sugar.

3. Put the non-dairy milk and acid (if using) into a separate bowl or large jug, then add the oil and whisk together.

4. If you're making the red velvet cupcakes, put the flavour agents into a blender with the milk and oil mixture and blend together.

5. Make a well in the centre of the dry ingredients, then add the wet ingredients and the flavour agents. Stir together using a spatula until just combined.

6. Pour the batter into the paper cases until each one is three-quarters full. Bake in the preheated oven for 20 to 25 minutes, rotating the tray halfway through the cooking time. Bake until the centre bounces back when pressed lightly and a skewer inserted into the centre comes out clean. Allow to cool completely on a wire rack before adding the frosting on top.

RECIPE:	VANILLA CUPCAKES	RED VELVET CUPCAKES	COURGETTE AND LIME CUPCAKES
FLOUR	270g plain white flour	250g plain white flour	300g plain white flour
RAISING AGENTS	3 tsp baking powder	4 tsp baking powder	1½ tsp baking powder ½ tsp bread soda
SWEETENER	230g coconut sugar/ caster sugar/xylitol	230g coconut sugar/ caster sugar/xylitol	200g coconut sugar/ caster sugar/xylitol
NON-DAIRY MILK	200ml non-dairy milk	200ml non-dairy milk	300ml non-dairy milk
ACID			Juice of 2 limes
OIL	200ml neutral-tasting oil	200ml neutral-tasting oil	200ml neutral-tasting oil
FLAVOUR AGENTS	1 tsp vanilla extract	150g beetroot, cooked and grated (p. 298) 5 tbsp cocoa powder 1 tsp pure vanilla extract	100g grated courgette Zest of 2 limes Zest of 1 lemon
FROSTING	Half of the white vanilla buttercream (p. 290)	Half of the white vanilla or pink buttercream (p. 290)	Half of the lemon and lime cream cheese frosting (p. 289)

BREAKDOWN

CAKES

Makes 1 double-decker cake

Once you master these easy recipes, you will have a really good understanding of how to make a wonderful vegan sponge that is light and fluffy with an excellent crumb. We have focused on three classic cakes, all based around a simple sponge cake, but they can be adapted in infinite ways. They all just need a good dollop of frosting or cream to dress them up so that they look like proper showstoppers!

1. Preheat the oven to 180°C fan/400°F/gas 6. Grease and line 2 × 20cm springform cake tins with non-stick baking paper.

2. If you're making the Victoria sponge cake, put the tins of coconut milk for the frosting into the fridge to allow the cream to separate and harden.

3. Mix all the dry ingredients together in a bowl, then sift them through a fine mesh sieve into a separate large bowl. Make a well in the centre.

4. Mix all the wet ingredients together, then add to the well in the centre of the dry ingredients. Using a spatula or a hand mixer, mix together until just combined.

5. Divide the mixture evenly between the two tins and bake in the preheated oven for 30 minutes (45 minutes for the carrot cake), rotating the tins halfway through the cooking time to ensure they cook evenly. When done, a skewer inserted into the centre should come out clean – if not, they need to go back in the oven for a little longer, until the skewer comes out dry. Remove the cakes from the oven and set aside on a wire rack to cool in the tins for 10 minutes before turning out and allowing to cool completely before frosting.

6. To assemble the chocolate fudge cake or carrot cake, put one cooled cake on a cake stand or serving plate and add half the frosting to the top of the cake. Working your way out from the centre, spread it evenly but not all the way to the edge, leaving about 1cm clear. Place the second cake on top, pressing it down lightly so the filling just comes to the edge. Add the top layer of frosting to the top of the cake, again working your way from the centre to spread the frosting all the way to the edge. Add the suggested decoration and cut into slices to serve.

7. If you're making the Victoria sponge cake, remove the tins of chilled coconut milk from the fridge, taking care not to shake the tins. Spoon off the hardened cream at the top of the tins and place in a bowl with the maple syrup and vanilla, mixing until smooth but being careful not to overmix, otherwise it can start to clump and slightly curdle.

8. Put one cooled cake on a cake stand or serving plate and add the jam filling to the top of the cake, spreading it evenly but not all the way to the edge, leaving about 1cm clear. Add half the cream, then, working your way out from the centre, spread it nearly to the edge in an even layer. Place the second cake on top, pressing it down lightly so the filling just comes to the edge. Then add your top layer of cream to the top of the cake, again working your way from the centre, spreading the cream to the edge. Add the suggested decoration and cut into slices to serve.

RECIPE:	VICTORIA SPONGE CAKE	CHOCOLATE FUDGE CAKE	CARROT CAKE
DRY INGREDIENTS			
FLOUR	400g plain white flour	320g plain white flour	400g plain white flour
SWEETENER	300g caster sugar	300g caster sugar	150g coconut sugar 150g caster sugar
FLAVOUR AGENT		80g cocoa powder	
RAISING AGENTS	2 tbsp baking powder ½ tsp baking soda	2 tbsp baking powder ½ tsp baking soda	2 tbsp baking powder 1 tsp baking soda
SPICES			1 tsp ground cinnamon 1 tsp allspice
WET INGREDIENTS			
NON-DAIRY MILK	200ml unsweetened almond milk	200ml unsweetened almond milk	200ml unsweetened almond milk
OIL	200ml neutral-tasting oil	250ml neutral-tasting oil	250ml neutral-tasting oil
FLAVOUR AGENTS	1 tsp vanilla extract	1 tsp vanilla extract	200g grated carrots 100g chopped walnuts 100g raisins 1 tsp vanilla extract
ACID	1 tbsp apple cider vinegar	1 tbsp apple cider vinegar	1 tbsp apple cider vinegar

BREAKDOWN ↑ ↓

RECIPES AND BREAKDOWN CONTINUE ON OPPOSITE PAGE

RECISE: *CONTINUED*	VICTORIA SPONGE CAKE	CHOCOLATE FUDGE CAKE	CARROT CAKE
FROSTING, FILLING AND DECORATION			
FROSTING / CREAM	2 × 400ml tins of full-fat coconut milk 1 tbsp maple syrup ½ tsp vanilla essence	1 batch of chocolate buttercream (p. 290)	1 batch of cream cheese frosting (p. 289)
FILLING	100g raspberry jam		
DECORATION	Fresh berries	Dark chocolate shavings	Walnuts

BREAKDOWN CONTINUED

FROSTING

Buttercream frosting is typically made up of two or three parts icing sugar to one part butter, which is not the healthiest food choice! So we had a little dilemma: do we try to make a healthier version, which wouldn't really deliver on taste, or do we go all out in an effort to make vegan frostings that are fluffy and soft, hold up well after being piped and taste and look just as good as the non-vegan kind? After about ten trials of a cashew-based frosting, we found them to be poor alternatives to their conventional counterparts, often lacking that indulgent quality, so we abandoned the mission and decided to go for two basic frostings: a vegan cream cheese frosting and a buttercream! We did dial back the amount of sweetener slightly compared to a typical buttercream, but these are still very much a treat and not something to be eaten regularly.

CREAM CHEESE FROSTING

*Makes enough for 1 double-decker cake
or 24 cupcakes*

RECIPE:	CREAM CHEESE FROSTING	MATCHA CREAM CHEESE FROSTING	LEMON AND LIME CREAM CHEESE FROSTING
ICING SUGAR	150g icing sugar	150g icing sugar	150g icing sugar
FAT	450g vegan cream cheese 125g coconut oil, melted	450g vegan cream cheese 125g coconut oil, melted	450g vegan cream cheese 125g coconut oil, melted
FLAVOUR AGENTS		2 tsp matcha green tea powder 1 tsp spirulina powder	Zest of 2 limes Zest of 1 lemon 1 tsp vanilla extract

(Left column label: BREAKDOWN ↑ ↓)

1. Sift the icing sugar into a large bowl. Add the fat and flavour agents (if using). Using a hand mixer or wooden spoon, mix until well combined.

2. Place the frosting in the fridge for 1 hour to firm up. Before using, stir again to loosen before piping or spreading on to your cooled cakes or cupcakes. The frosting can be made ahead and will keep in the fridge for up to 10 days.

BUTTERCREAM FROSTING

Makes enough for 1 double-decker cake
or 24 cupcakes

RECIPE:	WHITE VANILLA BUTTERCREAM	WHITE CHOCOLATE BUTTERCREAM	CHOCOLATE BUTTERCREAM	PINK BUTTERCREAM
FAT	250g coconut oil	150g cacao butter 150g coconut oil	150g coconut oil	200g coconut oil
SWEETENER	400g icing sugar	375g icing sugar	225g icing sugar	400g icing sugar
FLAVOUR AGENT	1 tsp vanilla extract	1 tsp vanilla extract	300g dark chocolate, chopped	2 tbsp beet juice

(left margin: BREAKDOWN ↑ ↓)

1. Gently melt the fat in a medium-sized saucepan set on a medium heat. If making the chocolate version, put the coconut oil and chocolate in a heatproof bowl over a pan of gently simmering water, ensuring the water doesn't touch the bottom of the bowl, and allow them to gently melt together. Remove from the heat.

2. Sift the sweetener into the pan or bowl, then stir in the flavour agent. (For the pink butter cream you can make your own beet juice, if needed, by peeling and grating ½ a beetroot, putting it in a colander over a bowl and squeezing out the juice by hand.) Beat together using a hand mixer or a whisk. Leave to set in a cool location (not a fridge as it will be too cold) for 20–30 minutes, until the frosting is firm enough to pipe.

3. The frosting will keep in the fridge for up to 10 days. Remove from the fridge and allow to come back to room temperature to make it spreadable.

RAINBOW CHEESECAKE

This recipe is inspired by a wonderful company in the Netherlands called Sharp Sharp that makes the most beautiful vegan cheesecakes, which they sell all over the country. The basic idea is to make one base layer, then mix and match any two cheesecake flavours from the framework on top. Some of our favourite combinations are:

- Mint chocolate: One mint and one chocolate layer

- Mocha: One chocolate and one coffee layer

- Berry lemony: One berry and one lemon layer

- Purple vanilla: One purple and one vanilla layer

1. Soak 125g of cashews for each cheesecake layer in two separate bowls overnight, then drain and rinse well. (If you don't have time to soak the cashews overnight, simply boil them for 10 minutes to soften, drain and rinse, and they will blend more easily.)

2. Line a 28cm × 20cm × 3cm baking tray with non-stick baking paper.

3. To make the base layer, blend the nuts in a food processor until they reach a breadcrumb-like texture, then add the rest of the base layer ingredients and blend for 1 to 3 minutes, until it all comes together. Transfer to the lined tray and spread out evenly, then pat down firmly so that it's firm, super smooth and level. Compacting it firmly will ensure that it will hold together when it's cut, and spreading it out evenly will result in lovely clear divisions between the layers. Chill in the fridge for 20 minutes or the freezer for 10 minutes.

4. Meanwhile, to make the first cheesecake layer, put the soaked and drained cashews, fat, sweetener and liquid in a food processor and blend on a medium to high speed for 5 minutes, until silky smooth. Add the flavour agents and blend again to combine. If you're making the chocolate cheesecake, first melt the chocolate in a heatproof bowl set over a pan of gently simmering water, making sure the water doesn't touch the bottom of the bowl, and allow to cool slightly before adding to the food processor and blending with the vanilla.

5. Spread this first cheesecake layer evenly on top of the chilled base layer, then place in the fridge for 2 hours or for 30 minutes in the freezer, until set firm. Meanwhile, repeat the steps above to make your second cheesecake layer.

6. Once the first layer is set, spread the second layer evenly on top and again place in the fridge for 2 hours or for 30 minutes in the freezer, until set firm.

7. If you like, you can decorate the top of the cheesecake once the second layer has set. Some of our favourite decorations are:

    - Blended or chopped goji berries
    - Desiccated coconut
    - Chopped cacao nibs
    - Cocoa powder
    - Freeze-dried strawberries or raspberries
    - Chocolate shavings

8. Cut the cheesecake into your desired serving size, which could be small petit fours or larger squares. The cheesecake is best served straight from the fridge, as too much warmth will make it runny. The cheesecake will keep in the fridge for up to 5 days.

RECIPE:	VANILLA	PURPLE	MINT
CASHEWS	125g cashews	125g cashews	125g cashews
BASE LAYER	75g cashews 75g almonds 50g pitted dates 1 tbsp coconut oil 1½ tsp vanilla extract	75g cashews 75g almonds 50g pitted dates 1 tbsp coconut oil 1½ tsp vanilla extract	75g cashews 75g almonds 50g pitted dates 1 tbsp coconut oil 1½ tsp vanilla extract
FAT	100g coconut oil 30g coconut cream	100g coconut oil 30g coconut cream	100g coconut oil 30g coconut cream
SWEETENER	50ml maple syrup	50ml maple syrup	50ml maple syrup
LIQUID	4 tbsp water	150ml water	4 tbsp water
FLAVOUR AGENTS	1 tsp vanilla extract	60g frozen acai berries or 1 tsp acai powder	¾ tsp peppermint oil ¾ tsp spirulina powder

BREAKDOWN ↑ ↓

RECIPE:	CHOCOLATE	LEMON	BERRY	COFFEE
CASHEWS	125g cashews	125g cashews	125g cashews	125g cashews
BASE LAYER	75g cashews 75g almonds 50g pitted dates 1 tbsp coconut oil 1½ tsp vanilla extract	75g cashews 75g almonds 50g pitted dates 1 tbsp coconut oil 1½ tsp vanilla extract	75g cashews 75g almonds 50g pitted dates 1 tbsp coconut oil 1½ tsp vanilla extract	75g cashews 75g almonds 50g pitted dates 1 tbsp coconut oil 1½ tsp vanilla extract
FAT	50g coconut oil	100g coconut oil 30g coconut cream	100g coconut oil 30g coconut cream	100g coconut oil 30g coconut cream
SWEETENER	25ml maple syrup	50ml maple syrup	50ml maple syrup	50ml maple syrup
LIQUID	4 tsp water		150ml water	2 tbsp water
FLAVOUR AGENTS	75g dark chocolate, chopped ½ tsp vanilla extract	4 tbsp lemon juice 2 tsp lemon zest ⅛ tsp ground turmeric	30g frozen raspberries 30g frozen strawberries ½ tsp beet powder (optional)	3 to 4 tbsp brewed coffee

BREAKDOWN

Essentials and Extras

This chapter is where we've put together some essential how-tos for cooking methods that are used or mentioned throughout this book, including how to roast veg, toast nuts and seeds, cook beans from scratch, make a flax or chia 'egg' and make vegetable stock. Once you've got a handle on those fundamentals, you can take things to the next level by making your own pickled veg, seed mixes, dips and condiments.

ESSENTIALS

HOW TO COOK VEG

Peel your veg and chop into the size you need for your recipe. Coat with a couple of tablespoons of oil and a good pinch of salt, then spread out on one or two baking trays in an even layer so that nothing is covering anything else – you want there to be enough space between them to allow the air to circulate. Roast in the oven until soft, golden around the edges and delicious. The oil helps the veg reach a higher temperature when cooking and creates a more even caramelization of the veg. You can use a little less oil if you're watching calories.

Here are some more specific instructions for roasting or cooking veg that are used in recipes throughout the book, but still follow the guidelines above for coating in oil and salt and spreading out in a single layer, spaced well apart, on a baking tray.

- **Aubergines:** Roast in the oven at 200°C fan/425°F/gas 7 for 25 to 30 minutes. You want to make sure you cook them until they are super soft, with a melt-in-your-mouth texture.

- **Beetroot:** Roast in the oven at 180°C fan/400°F/gas 6 for 25 minutes, until soft and cooked through.

- **Butternut and other squash:** Roast in the oven at 180°C fan/400°F/gas 6 for 25 minutes, until soft and cooked through.

- **Carrots:** To roast, bake in the oven at 180°C fan/400°F/gas 6 for approx. 25 minutes, until soft and cooked through. To boil, add to a pot of salted boiling water, reduce the heat and simmer for 15 minutes.

- **Cauliflower:** Roast in the oven at 200°C fan/425°F/gas 7 for 20 minutes, until soft and starting to char at the edges.

- **Celeriac:** To roast, bake in the oven at 180°C fan/400°F/gas 6 for approx. 25 minutes, until soft and cooked through. To boil, add to a pot of salted boiling water, reduce the heat and simmer for 15 minutes.

- **Courgettes:** Roast in the oven at 200°C fan/425°F/gas 7 for about 20 to 25 minutes, until they start to really char and caramelize.

- **Garlic:** Cut the top off the head of garlic, leaving the tips of the cloves exposed. Place on a baking tray and roast in the oven at 180°C fan/400°F/gas 6 for 15 to 20 minutes, until soft.

- **Kale:** To steam kale, place it in a steamer and steam for about 5 minutes, until it's nice and soft, with a melt-in-your-mouth texture.

- **Leeks:** Roast in the oven at 180°C fan/400°F/gas 6 for 15 to 20 minutes, until they start to caramelize and become sweet, succulent and super tasty. When roasting leeks, make sure to include the green part of the leek too, as this crisps up wonderfully, but make sure you give it a good clean first, as soil is often hiding inside. Add a couple of tablespoons of water along with the oil to the baking tray to steam the leeks so that they become more succulent.

- **Mushrooms:** To pan-fry, heat 2 tablespoons of oil in a wide-bottomed frying pan on a medium to high heat. Add your prepped mushrooms and cook for 5 to 8 minutes, until they wilt down quite dramatically in size and start to char on the edges. To roast, coat with 1 tablespoon of tamari or soy sauce as well as the oil and roast in the oven at 200°C fan/425°F/gas 7 for approx. 15 minutes, until they start to crisp up.

- **Parsnips:** To roast, bake in the oven at 180°C fan/400°F/gas 6 for approx. 25 minutes, until soft and cooked through. To boil, add to a pot of salted boiling water, reduce the heat and simmer for 15 minutes.

- **Pumpkin:** Roast in the oven at 180°C fan/400°F/gas 6 for 25 to 30 minutes, until softened and starting to brown at the edges.

- **Red onions:** Roast in the oven at 200°C fan/425°F/gas 7 for 15 to 20 minutes, until starting to char a little.

- **Red or yellow peppers:** Roast your deseeded and prepped peppers in the oven at 200°C fan/425°F/gas 7 for 25 to 30 minutes, until they start to char at the edges and smell fab! (Whole peppers will take a few minutes longer.)

- **Sweet potatoes:** To roast, bake in the oven at 180°C fan/400°F/gas 6 for approx. 25 minutes, until softened and starting to crisp on the outside.

HOW TO COOK GRAINS

- **Bulghur wheat:** Combine 1 part bulghur wheat with 2 parts water and a pinch of salt in a saucepan. Bring to the boil, then cover the pan, reduce the heat and simmer for about 12 minutes, until all the water has evaporated and the bulghur is tender. Drain off any excess water, then fluff up the bulghur with a fork.

- **Couscous:** We prefer to use wholemeal couscous, as it's much higher in fibre than normal couscous or white couscous. Put the couscous into a large heatproof bowl with a pinch of salt and maybe some other spices too, such as ground cumin, freshly ground black pepper or paprika to give it a red colour. If you want to make it richer, add 1 or 2 tablespoons of olive oil and mix well. Cover the couscous with just-boiled water from the kettle until the water goes just above the level of the couscous, approx. 1cm above the surface. Cover the top of the bowl with a plate and let it sit for 5 minutes, until the couscous has absorbed all the water. Remove the plate and break up with a fork until it's soft and fluffy.

- **Quinoa:** Nutty and sweet, quinoa is a pseudo-grain, as it's actually a seed (which is why it's high in fibre and protein, like most seeds). To cook, combine 1 part quinoa with 2 parts water and a pinch of salt in a saucepan. Bring to the boil on a high heat, uncovered, then reduce the heat to medium to maintain a gentle simmer. Cook for about 15 minutes, until the quinoa has absorbed all the water (small amounts of quinoa will be ready closer to 10 minutes; larger amounts may take 15 to 20 minutes). Remove the pot from the heat, cover with a lid and let the quinoa steam for 5 minutes. This step gives the quinoa time to pop open. Remove the lid and fluff up the quinoa with a fork.

- **Rice (white, brown and red):** Combine 1 part rice with 2 parts water and a pinch of salt in a saucepan. Bring to the boil on a high heat, then reduce the heat to low to medium to maintain a gentle simmer. Cook, uncovered, for about 30 minutes in total, until the rice has absorbed all the water. Remove the pot from the heat, cover with a lid and let the rice sit for 5 minutes to give the rice time to fluff up. Remove the lid and fluff up the rice with a fork.

HOW TO TOAST NUTS AND SEEDS

Toasting nuts and seeds is such a simple thing to do and it really enhances and intensifies their flavour. Put them into a hot, dry frying pan on a medium heat and toast for 5 to 8 minutes, stirring or shaking the pan occasionally, until they start to turn golden. Keep a close eye on them to make sure they don't burn. Tip them out on to a plate so that they don't continue to cook in the residual heat of the pan, and set aside to cool. Alternatively you can bake them in a preheated oven at 180°C fan/400°F/gas 6 for 10 to 15 minutes until they start to turn golden.

HOW TO COOK BEANS AND LENTILS FROM SCRATCH

When going to the trouble of soaking and boiling beans we often cook a large volume, as they will last for 3 or 4 days when kept in the fridge and they can be frozen too.

The first step when cooking dried beans is to give them a good rinse to remove any dust or debris, then to put them into a large bowl and cover them with cold water to soak overnight. They will double in volume when soaked, so make sure you use a bowl that's big enough.

The next day, drain and rinse the beans, then transfer them to a large pot. Fill the pot with water until it's two-thirds full. The extra space is to make it easier when boiling, as some beans, such as chickpeas, often froth a little, so this extra space will help to minimize the mess!

Bring to the boil, then reduce the heat and simmer for anywhere from 1 to 3 hours (see below for more accurate cooking times), until tender and soft but still holding their shape – you don't want them to be mushy and falling apart. We always keep the water from cooking beans to use as a stock for sauces or soups.

- Black beans: approx. 90 minutes

- Butter beans: approx. 90 minutes

- Chickpeas: 1 to 3 hours, depending on the amount you are boiling

- Kidney beans: 1½ to 2 hours

- Lentils: 35 to 60 minutes

Should you use bread soda (bicarbonate of soda) when cooking beans?

Some people say that you can't achieve a soft enough bean without adding bread soda while they're cooking, but we've soaked and cooked beans for over a decade now in our cafés and we have never used bread soda. However, it's often used with old beans to soften the skins or to possibly speed up the cooking process a little – bread soda makes the water more alkaline, which makes it more conducive to cooking a softer bean. If you know you've got older beans or if you need them to cook faster, use ¼ teaspoon of bread soda per 450g of dried beans.

HOW TO MAKE A FLAX OR CHIA 'EGG'

You can use a flax or chia 'egg' to replace hen's eggs as a binder in vegan cooking. If you use ground chia seeds, then a flax 'egg' and chia 'egg' can be used interchangeably.

- Flax 'egg': Soak 1 tablespoon of ground flax seeds in 3 tablespoons of water and leave to coagulate for 5 minutes or so. The ground flax will soak up all the liquid and form a gloopy, glue-like consistency that works perfectly as a binder. We use them in our burgers, pancakes and in lots of our baking.

- Chia 'egg': Soak 1 tablespoon of ground or whole chia seeds in 3 tablespoons of water and leave to coagulate for 5 minutes or so. While it isn't necessary to grind the chia seeds, if you leave them whole it means the grey speckles will be visible throughout whatever you are making. As above, we use chia 'eggs' in baking, to bind our burgers and often in our pancake batter too.

HOW TO MAKE VEGETABLE STOCK

We make our own vegetable stock in our cafés, as it uses a lot of the veg offcuts that would otherwise be wasted. Making stock is basically like making tea – it's about getting flavour into water. Plus making your own stock is a lot more flavourful and less expensive than ready-made stock bought from the shop. Instead of giving you a recipe to follow verbatim, we wanted to give you our veg stock basics so that you can see for yourself that it's much simpler to make than you might think.

Start by saving your veg offcuts – making stock is a great way to use all the vegetable trimmings that would otherwise be thrown into the bin. Freezing veg trimmings and scraps in an airtight container or freezer-proof bag is a great habit to get into, as then you'll have a stockpile ready for when you need it. We usually include carrot tops, onion and garlic skins, herb stalks, as well as seeds from pumpkins and squashes. Just make sure they are all clean and free of rot or mould.

Stock is also a great way of using up veg that are past their best: rubbery carrots, wilted spring onions, half a soft onion, a few random cloves of garlic in the fridge door or some sad-looking herbs. We also add herbs and spices such as bay leaves, cinnamon sticks, mustard seeds, juniper berries, coriander seeds and peppercorns. Seaweed is great too, as it will really amp up the nutritional and mineral element of your soup. Kombu works particularly well.

Put all these into a stockpot with plenty of fresh cold water and bring to the boil, then reduce to a gentle simmer. Cook for about 1 hour, which is usually enough time for the flavours to infuse into the water. The longer you leave it, the more flavoursome and more concentrated the stock gets as the water evaporates, giving you a stronger stock.

Take the pot off the stove and remove all the vegetables with a slotted spoon or set a strainer over a big bowl and pour the stock through. Divide the stock between storage containers, then allow to cool completely before storing in the fridge or freezer. If freezing, make sure you put a label and the date on the bag. Vegetable stock will keep for 3 to 4 days in the fridge and 6 months in the freezer.

What not to include in veg stock

There are a few things that you should avoid including in your stock:

- Cruciferous veg or brassicas (broccoli, cauliflower, cabbage). These contain sulphur, which gives off an overly dominant flavour. Plus these veg make the broth bitter and make it smell unpleasant.

- Beetroot. It will turn your stock pink, so don't add it unless you want a pink soup!

- Onion skins. Avoid too many of these, as they will make your stock brown.

- Mediterranean veg. We never use veg like peppers, aubergines or courgettes, as they don't really break down or add any flavours to the stock.

- Potatoes. They give off too much starch.

- Rosemary or sage. Strong flavoured herbs like these can overpower the stock.

- Spices. We usually don't include chilli (unless we're making a spicy soup), curry powder, turmeric or cumin seeds.

EXTRAS

Little extras like pickled veg or a seed mix will elevate your salads, while dips such as hummus and tapenade are a great way to add more flavour to any sandwich, smörgåsbord or picnic, to round out a dinner or serve with crackers or raw veggies as a nibble to have with drinks. Condiments can be the difference between a good sandwich and a great one. We grew up eating ham and cheese sandwiches every day for lunch at school and college and would add some crisps when the bread was particularly hard, but today our kids use hummus instead of butter and pesto is the new ham!

QUICK PICKLED VEG

Pickling transforms veg by using an acid to soften them while also adding sharpness and colour. For example, by pickling red onions, the strong flavour is mellowed out and they turn a bright pink colour. Pickling is also a great way of preserving fresh veg. Simply create a pickling brine by combining equal parts water and vinegar, season with spices, salt and pepper, and leave your veg to pickle for anywhere from a few minutes to a few days or up to a few months in the fridge.

One of the keys to pickling quickly is that your veg are finely or thinly chopped so that the vinegar can quickly soften and flavour them. Most vinegars work well, but it's best to avoid aged or concentrated vinegars, such as malt vinegar or balsamic.

The best way to add more flavour is to add herbs or spices to your pickling brine. Here are some of our favourites:

- Fresh or dried herbs, such as oregano, thyme, rosemary and dill

- Fresh chopped garlic

- Fresh ginger or turmeric to add a more Eastern note

- Whole spices such as fennel, cumin, coriander and mustard seeds, star anise and peppercorns all work great

- Ground spices, including turmeric, cumin, coriander, smoked paprika, or just about any other spice that takes your fancy

Makes 1 x 250g jar

1. Prepare your veg:

    - **Pickled red onions:** Peel the red onion and cut it in half, then slice into thin half-moons.

    - **Asian-style pickled carrot strips:** Peel the carrot into long, thin strips. Peel and finely chop the garlic and ginger. Deseed the red chilli and finely chop (or include the seeds for a hotter pickle) or leave it out altogether.

    - **Pickled pink fennel with cumin:** Slice the fennel bulb very thinly (a mandoline works well for this). If you can't source beet juice, make your own by peeling and grating ½ a beetroot, then put it in a colander set over a bowl and use your hands to squeeze out the juice. Crush the peppercorns in a pestle and mortar.

    - **Pickled garlicky mangetout with thyme:** Slice the mangetout open. Peel and finely chop the garlic.

2. To make the pickling solution, put the vinegar, water and flavour agents, spices and seasoning into a sterilized jar and stir to combine, then add the prepared veg.

3. Allow to sit for as little as 10 minutes or as long as a couple of months in the fridge. The longer you leave it, the stronger the flavour will be.

4. Each of these pickles will keep in a sealed jar in the fridge for a number of months.

RECIPE:	PICKLED RED ONIONS	ASIAN-STYLE PICKLED CARROT STRIPS	PICKLED PINK FENNEL WITH CUMIN	PICKLED GARLICKY MANGETOUT WITH THYME
VEG	1 red onion	1 carrot	1 fennel bulb	100g mangetout
VINEGAR	100ml apple cider vinegar	100ml apple cider vinegar	100ml rice vinegar	100ml mirin or rice vinegar
WATER	100ml water	100ml water	100ml water	100ml water
FLAVOUR AGENTS	Pinch of salt	1 garlic clove 1 fresh red chilli ½ × thumb-size piece of fresh ginger 1 tsp ground turmeric ½ tsp salt	2 tbsp beet juice 3 black peppercorns ½ tsp cumin seeds ½ tsp salt	2 garlic cloves 2 tsp dried thyme 1 tsp salt

BREAKDOWN ↑ ↓

SEED MIXES

By toasting nuts or seeds, some of the moisture is evaporated and the flavour intensifies through caramelization. Add a generous serving of salt, and boom, an instant hit of flavour and added texture.

RECIPE:	GOMASHIO	DUKKAH	ZA'ATAR
NUTS		50g hazelnuts	50g pine nuts
SEEDS	50g sesame seeds (use black and/or white)	2 tbsp sesame seeds	2 tbsp sesame seeds
SPICES		1 tsp fennel seeds 1 tsp cumin seeds 1 tsp coriander seeds	2 tbsp dried oregano 1 tbsp cumin seeds 1 tbsp coriander seeds 1 tbsp sumac Pinch of chilli flakes
SALT	Generous pinch of salt	Generous pinch of salt	Generous pinch of salt

↑ **BREAKDOWN** ↓

Makes approx. 60g

1. Roughly chop the nuts (if using) into smaller pieces so that they will toast better, or briefly pulse in a food processor.

2. Toast the chopped nuts, the seeds and any whole spices (such as fennel, cumin and coriander seeds) in a hot, dry pan on a high heat for 6 to 8 minutes, stirring or shaking the pan occasionally and taking care that they don't burn, until golden and fragrant and the whole spices are starting to pop. Alternatively, you can put them on a baking tray and toast them in an oven preheated to 180°C fan/400°F/gas 6 for 8 to 10 minutes, until golden and fragrant.

3. Allow to cool, then transfer to a pestle and mortar, add a generous pinch of salt and grind together until everything has broken down into crumbs, but with a few larger pieces so that you still have a little bite. Alternatively, you could put everything into a sealed ziplock bag and bash with a rolling pin.

4. Store in a sealed jar in a cool, dark place for up to 3 months.

5. These work well as a garnish to elevate a soup, salad, curry or Buddha bowl.

HUMMUS

Now that it's found in most stores, it's hard to remember a time when hummus was seen as exotic fare. Hummus is a daily go-to in a vegan diet. It's a great substitute for butter and we eat it with nearly everything. Steve's two-and-a-half-year-old son Ned will often even have a hummus-filled pitta after his porridge! We love it so much that we make literally tonnes of our own hummus (a classic and a beetroot version) each week and sell it in supermarkets all over Ireland. But when it comes to hummus, there's the good, the bad and the ugly. It can range from a bland, pale dip with a dubious texture to heavenly when made properly and perfectly seasoned.

THE ESSENTIALS

Chickpeas: In an ideal world we would all soak and cook dried chickpeas from scratch (see p. 302 if you'd like to know how), but tinned or jarred cooked chickpeas are a lot more practical, convenient and quick. Jarred cooked chickpeas normally contain bigger, creamier chickpeas that will give you a wonderfully smooth, creamy hummus, but the jars are more expensive than tins. When using tinned chickpeas, we try to use organic where possible.

Alternatively, virtually any type of cooked bean can be used to make hummus. One of our favourites is butter beans, which have a buttery texture that makes a smooth, creamy hummus, but you can use kidney beans, black beans, cannellini beans, pinto beans or black-eyed peas as well.

Tahini: Tahini is a Middle Eastern paste made from ground sesame seeds. There are two types: dark tahini and light tahini. Dark tahini includes the hulls (the outer protective layer) of the sesame seeds, resulting in a much more earthy and darker tahini that will make your hummus a darker colour too. Light tahini is made using just the sesame seeds, with the hulls removed. In our opinion it's tastier than dark tahini, with a sweeter, less earthy flavour. We use light tahini in all our hummus. If you want to get a little creative or if tahini is hard to find in your local store, you can easily replace the tahini with your favourite nut or seed butter, such as almond butter, peanut butter or pumpkin seed butter, which will also give your hummus a more distinctive flavour.

Oil: When we first started making hummus about 15 years ago we thought that oil would just thin it out, but in fact it gives hummus a pillowy, creamy texture. We prefer to use a light-tasting olive oil that's not too acidic or a neutral-tasting sunflower oil, which allows the other flavours in the hummus to come through.

However, oil is also an opportunity to add another flavour dimension to your hummus if desired. For example, sesame oil will complement the tahini and intensify the sesame notes, while an infused oil, such as chilli oil or oil left over from soaking olives or cooking artichokes, will add another subtle layer of flavour. Or just use your favourite walnut or avocado oil to add another dimension.

Garlic: If you find raw garlic a little too strong, try roasting it first to mellow the flavour (see p. 298) or use a little dried garlic powder. If using dried garlic powder, use approx. ½ teaspoon of dried garlic to replace 1 small clove of fresh garlic. Hummus still works without any garlic at all, but you may have to add other spices, such as cumin, to make up for its absence so that it isn't too bland.

Lemon juice: We like to use fresh lemon juice in our hummus, but you can easily use lime juice, orange juice, grapefruit juice or any other acid, such as your favourite vinegar. Lemon will add a vibrant citrus acidity, but other forms of acid will work well and will enable you to make a more personalized hummus. However, if you use a dark vinegar, such as balsamic vinegar, it will also affect the colour of your hummus.

Salt: Always season to taste and start by under-seasoning, but the recipe will also provide a good guideline.

There are many different types of salt that you can use to incorporate different flavours into your hummus, such as seaweed salt, sulphur salt to add an eggy note or even truffle salt to add a sweet mushroom flavour. Alternatively, if you're getting really experimental, you can add the salty component with something that also has umami properties, such as miso, tamari or soy sauce. Your hummus will be a little out there, but it can also be incredibly tasty!

Spices and extras: Hummus purists wouldn't add any spices, but nowadays hummus is free game and you can find anything from chilli hummus or sun-dried tomato hummus to curry hummus. Noel Healy, one of our chefs many years ago, used to swear by a little smoked paprika, while Dorene Palmer, our chef 'mom', used to love serving it with some fresh parsley, a pinch of sweet paprika and an extra drizzle of olive oil. See p. 316 for some of the more creative versions that we love.

BASIC HUMMUS

Makes 450g

Hummus can be quite personal. Our kids love a gentle, creamy hummus; we love a strong hummus with cumin, lemon and lots of garlic; and our brother Darragh loves his hummus packed so full of tahini that it's as thick as tile grout! Once you've mastered the basic hummus framework below, the options to make it your own and customize it to your taste are limited only by your imagination.

1. Drain and rinse the chickpeas. Peel and chop the garlic.

2. Put all the ingredients into a food processor and blend until nice and smooth. Check the texture and blend in another 2 tablespoons of water if the consistency is too thick for your liking.

3. Taste and adjust the seasoning with a little more salt or another squeeze of lemon if needed.

4. Store in an airtight container in the fridge for up to 1 week.

Light hummus: This hummus is pretty basic and is a favourite with kids, as it's very neutral-tasting yet reasonably well seasoned. It's also comparatively low-fat and is quite thin, not creamy. It doesn't have a strong tahini flavour.

Extra-thick hummus: We have added significantly more tahini in this version, similar to the amount used in parts of the Middle East. This makes a thick, paste-like hummus that's too thick for many people, but for others it's textural perfection! We also increased the amount of lemon juice to cut through the extra tahini, while the addition of ground cumin and chilli adds a subtle extra flavour.

Creamy hummus: This hummus uses a lot more oil, resulting in a creamier hummus, so we also increased the amount of lemon juice in this version to cut through the creaminess. This hummus shows the difference between fat coming from tahini and fat coming from oil. Tahini is a wholefood source of fat, as it contains fibre, whereas oil is a refined fat, which has no fibre. Oil will create a richer, creamier, more indulgent hummus, but it's also higher in fat.

RECIPE:	LIGHT HUMMUS	EXTRA-THICK HUMMUS	CREAMY HUMMUS
CHICKPEAS	1 × 400g tin of chickpeas	1 × 400g tin of chickpeas	1 × 400g tin of chickpeas
TAHINI	2 tbsp tahini	100g tahini	2 tbsp tahini
OIL	1 tbsp olive oil		4 tbsp olive oil
GARLIC	1 garlic clove	1 garlic clove	1 garlic clove
LEMON JUICE	1 tbsp lemon juice	Juice of 1 lemon (2 tbsp)	Juice of 1 lemon (2 tbsp)
SALT	1 tsp salt	1 tsp salt	1 tsp salt
SPICES		½ tsp ground cumin Pinch of ground chilli powder	
WATER	70ml water	50ml water	

BREAKDOWN

CREATIVE HUMMUS

Makes 500g

These recipes will give you a few ideas for the creative directions in which you can take your hummus.

1. Drain and rinse the chickpeas/beans. Peel and chop the garlic. Remove the leaves of the fresh herbs from their stalks (if using), then roughly chop the leaves and discard the stalks.

2. Put all the ingredients into a food processor (except for the cherry tomatoes if making the guacamole hummus) and blend until nice and smooth. Check the texture and blend in another 2 tablespoons of water if the consistency is too thick for your liking.

3. Taste and adjust the seasoning with a little more salt or another squeeze of lemon if needed.

4. Store in an airtight container in the fridge for up to 1 week.

RECIPE:	CARROT AND CORIANDER HUMMUS	BUTTER BEAN, PEA AND MINT HUMMUS	GUACAMOLE HUMMUS	ROASTED RED PEPPER AND PEANUT HUMMUS
CHICKPEAS / BEANS	1 × 400g tin of chickpeas	1 × 400g tin of butter beans	1 × 400g tin of chickpeas	1 × 400g tin of chickpeas
TAHINI / NUT BUTTER/ AVOCADO	3 tbsp light tahini	4 tbsp light tahini	1 large ripe avocado	3 tbsp smooth peanut butter
OIL	3 tbsp olive oil	3 tbsp olive oil	3 tbsp olive oil	3 tbsp olive oil
GARLIC	1 garlic clove	1 garlic clove	2 garlic cloves	1 garlic clove
LEMON JUICE	2 tbsp lemon juice	4 tbsp lemon juice	4 tbsp lemon juice	2 tbsp lemon juice
SALT	1 tsp salt	2 tsp salt	2 tsp salt	1 tsp salt
HERBS, SPICES AND EXTRAS	80g roasted carrots (p. 298) 15g fresh coriander	100g thawed frozen peas (50g blended through and 50g left whole) 10g fresh mint	15g fresh coriander 1 tsp ground cumin ½ tsp chilli powder 10 cherry tomatoes	80g roasted red peppers (p. 300) Pinch of smoked paprika
WATER	100ml water	50ml water	50ml water	50ml water

← BREAKDOWN →

TAPENADE

Makes 250g

Tapenade is an olive paste or spread found throughout the Mediterranean that is traditionally made by blending olives, capers, anchovies and olive oil. It can be served on crusty bread or toast, crackers or flatbreads, with raw veggies, as a salty condiment on sandwiches, or can be added to a vegan mezze platter for easy entertaining. When done right, tapenade can convert even the most ardent olive haters to olive lovers. The key is to use good olives – no amount of good cooking or blending can make a bad olive taste good.

1. Simply put all the ingredients into a food processor or blender, or use a pestle and mortar, and blend until smooth. If using a pestle and mortar, add all the ingredients except the olive oil and grind them together, then slowly add the oil until it comes together nicely.

2. Taste and adjust the seasoning with a little more salt or acid if needed.

3. Store in a sealed jar in the fridge for up to 1 week.

RECIPE:	KALAMATA TAPENADE	GREEN OLIVE TAPENADE	NIÇOISE OLIVE TAPENADE
OLIVES	200g pitted black Kalamata olives	200g pitted green olives	200g pitted black Niçoise olives
OLIVE OIL	3 tbsp olive oil	3 tbsp olive oil	3 tbsp olive oil
ACID		Zest of ½ a lemon	1 tsp red wine vinegar
FLAVOUR AGENTS	1 sprig of fresh thyme, leaves picked (optional) 1 tbsp capers	1 sprig of fresh oregano, leaves picked (optional) 1 tbsp capers	2 to 3 sun-dried tomatoes (optional) 1 tbsp capers
SEASONING (TO TASTE)	Salt and freshly ground black pepper	Salt and freshly ground black pepper	Salt and freshly ground black pepper

BREAKDOWN ↑ ↓

VEGAN MAYONNAISE

Makes 350ml

It's often thought that you need a degree in witchcraft to get a mayonnaise to emulsify, but the good news is that the vegan version is fool-proof and tastes just as good as the original, if not better. Conventional mayonnaise is made stable by using egg yolks combined with oil and lemon juice to create a wonderfully creamy sauce that is seasoned with mustard and salt. The key ingredients in our vegan mayo are equal parts soya milk and a neutral-tasting oil (in our recipe, 150ml of each) combined with 1 tablespoon of lemon juice. Soya milk has lecithin in it, which is often added as an emulsifier in chocolate to stop it going solid when it's being tempered. This lecithin helps the soya milk to combine and link with the oil, while the lemon juice makes it all emulsify. Here is a framework and some ideas of where you can take this magical emulsion.

If you're making the beetroot mayo and can't source beet juice, you can make your own by peeling and grating ½ a beetroot, then put it into a colander set over a bowl and use your hands to squeeze out the juice. You only want the juice for the mayo.

1. Put the soya milk, lemon juice, mustard or tamari/soy sauce, extras, garlic powder and seasoning into a blender or food processor and blend for 1 minute.

2. With the motor still running, slowly add the oil in a thin, steady stream until the mayo emulsifies. Taste and adjust the seasoning with more salt or lemon juice if needed. Store in a sealed jar in the fridge for up to 2 weeks.

RECIPE:	BASIC MAYO	ZINGY BASIL MAYO	BEETROOT MAYO	SPICY HARISSA MAYO	SWEET UMAMI MAYO
SOYA MILK	150ml soya milk	150ml soya milk	150ml soya milk	150ml soya milk	150ml soya milk
LEMON JUICE	1 tbsp lemon juice	1 tbsp lemon juice	1 tbsp lemon juice	1 tbsp lemon juice	1 tbsp lemon juice
MUSTARD OR TAMARI/ SOY SAUCE	½ tbsp Dijon mustard	½ tbsp Dijon mustard	½ tbsp Dijon mustard		2 tbsp tamari or soy sauce
EXTRAS		Zest of ½ a lemon 15g fresh basil, leaves stripped from the stalks	1 to 2 tbsp beet juice (see p. 320)	4 tbsp harissa (see p. 328) or more to taste	1 tbsp miso 1 tbsp maple syrup
GARLIC POWDER	½ tsp garlic powder	½ tsp garlic powder	½ tsp garlic powder	½ tsp garlic powder	½ tsp garlic powder
SEASONING (TO TASTE)	¼ tsp salt Freshly ground black pepper	¼ tsp salt Freshly ground black pepper	¼ tsp salt Freshly ground black pepper	¼ tsp salt Frehly ground black pepper	¼ tsp salt Freshly ground black pepper
OIL (USE A NEUTRAL-TASTING OIL SUCH AS SUNFLOWER, GROUNDNUT OR GRAPESEED)	150ml oil	150ml oil	150ml oil	150ml oil	150ml oil

← BREAKDOWN →

KETCHUP

Makes 500ml

Ketchup is so easy to make at home that you might not go back to your favourite store-bought brand. Ketchup is the perfect sauce to accompany our vegan fry-up in the Breakfast chapter (see pp. 58–69) and our burger and fries (see pp. 121 and 139). The perfect balance between acid and sweet, ketchup always tastes like more. The recipe framework below includes a simple basic version plus two variations if you feel like fancying it up!

1. Put all the ingredients into a blender (or put everything into a large jug and use a hand-held immersion blender) and blend until smooth. Or you can simply put everything in a bowl and whisk by hand.

2. Taste and adjust the seasoning with a little more salt or acid if needed.

3. Transfer to a jar or bottle and store in the fridge for up to 1 week.

RECIPE:	BASIC KETCHUP	SWEET CHILLI KETCHUP	BBQ KETCHUP
TOMATO	200g tomato purée	200g tomato purée	200g tomato purée
ACID	100ml apple cider vinegar	100ml apple cider vinegar	100ml apple cider vinegar
SWEETENER	100g maple or agave syrup	150g maple or agave syrup	100g maple or agave syrup
WATER	6 tbsp water	6 tbsp water	6 tbsp water
FLAVOUR AGENTS		½ to 1 tsp chilli flakes (depending on how spicy you like it)	2 tbsp tamari or soy sauce 2 tbsp maple syrup 1 tsp cayenne pepper 1 tsp Dijon mustard 1 tsp smoked paprika
SEASONING	1 tsp salt ¼ tsp freshly ground black pepper	1 tsp salt ¼ tsp freshly ground black pepper	

BREAKDOWN ↑ ↓

GUACAMOLE

Homemade guacamole is hard to beat and can be served as a dip with tortilla chips and salsa or used as a delicious component in a sandwich, burrito or salad. The key to a great guacamole is the quality and ripeness of the avocados you use – use ripe Hass avocados, as these are the creamiest kind – and getting the balance right between the acid, salt and fat.

Texture: First of all, do you like your guacamole chunky or smooth? We like it somewhere in the middle, so we use a fork to bring it all together, mashing some of the avocado to add body and to hold the whole chunks together.

Acid: In Mexican cooking acid typically comes from limes or bitter oranges, but lemons, blood oranges, grapefruit, pineapple, pomelos, pomegranate molasses and vinegar can all work too – it's your choice.

Extra fruit or veg: Tomatoes are the most common type of extra fruit used in guacamole, but sometimes we make it with mangoes, charred pineapple, peaches or even nectarines. The sweeter fruits contrast with the acid and help to really elevate and enliven the fat from the avocado.

Spices, herbs and chilli: Ground cumin, chilli (fresh, flakes or powder) and fresh coriander are often added. We've made guacamole with fresh mint or smoked paprika and charred red peppers, and aromatic spices such as cinnamon, ground cloves and even some grated dark chocolate work great in guacamole too.

1. If you're making the basic or smoky red pepper guacamole, deseed the chilli if you want to decrease the heat levels, then finely chop. If you're making the fruity and spicy guacamole, leave the chilli whole.

2. To prepare the extra fruit or veg, halve the cherry tomatoes or dice the roasted red peppers. If you're making the fruity and spicy guacamole, peel the pineapple and dice into small bite-size pieces, then fry in a splash of oil in a frying pan along with the whole chilli on a high heat until the pineapple starts to caramelize and turn golden brown and the chilli starts to char, then set aside to cool. When it's cool enough to handle, finely chop the chilli.

3. To prepare the flavour agents, peel and finely chop the onion and garlic. Finely chop the sun-dried tomatoes (if using, the easiest way to chop sun-dried tomatoes is using clean scissors).

4. Strip the leaves from the fresh herbs and discard the stalks, then finely chop the leaves.

5. Put all the ingredients except the avocado into a large bowl and mix together.

6. Cut the avocados in half and remove the stones, then scoop the flesh out from the skin. We like a quite chunky guacamole, so we roughly chop it, then stir it through the other ingredients. If you prefer a smooth guacamole, mash the avocado with a fork or blender until it's the texture you like, then stir it through.

7. Taste and adjust the seasoning with a little more salt or acid if needed. Guacamole is best served and eaten fresh.

RECIPE:	BASIC GUACAMOLE	FRUITY AND SPICY GUACAMOLE	SMOKY RED PEPPER GUACAMOLE
AVOCADOS	2 ripe Hass avocados	2 ripe Hass avocados	2 ripe Hass avocados 1 tbsp olive oil
CHILLI (OPTIONAL)	¼ of a fresh red chilli	1 fresh red chilli	½ a fresh red chilli
EXTRA FRUIT OR VEG	5 cherry tomatoes	½ a pineapple	1 roasted red pepper (see p. 300) or 50g roasted red peppers from a jar
FLAVOUR AGENTS	½ a small red onion 1 clove of garlic	½ a small red onion 1 clove of garlic	2 to 3 sun-dried tomatoes (not in oil) ½ a small red onion 1 clove of garlic
HERBS	10g fresh coriander	5g fresh mint	10g fresh coriander
ACID	Juice of 1 lime	Juice of ½ a lemon	Juice of 1 lime
SPICES AND SEASONING	½ tsp salt Freshly ground black pepper (to taste)	½ tsp salt Freshly ground black pepper (to taste)	½ tsp smoked paprika (optional) ½ tsp salt Pinch of ground cinnamon (optional)

BREAKDOWN ↑ ↓

HARISSA

Harissa is a rockin' hot paste with its roots in Tunisia and is widely used in other countries in North Africa. You are likely to find as many versions of it as you are people who make it, so there really is no one standard recipe. It's everything we wish a bottled hot sauce would be — robust with sweet and complex flavours, not just a sharp, vinegary bite. We like ours sweet, spicy and salty with some smoky undertones. It's a wonderful condiment to have on hand to add to sauces or soups to give more flavour and spice. Combined with some soft gentle flavours, such as mayo (see p. 320), it adds a serious punch to any sandwich.

10 fresh red chillies

12 sun-dried tomatoes (not the kind in oil – about 40g)

4 cloves of garlic, peeled

8 tbsp olive oil

3 tsp salt

2 tsp chilli flakes

Makes 150ml

1. Preheat the oven to 220°C fan/475°F/gas 9.

2. Chop the tops off the chillies and discard, then cut the chillies in half lengthways, leaving the seeds in. Place on a baking tray and roast in the preheated oven for 15 minutes.

3. Meanwhile, soak the sun-dried tomatoes in just-boiled water from the kettle for 5 minutes, then drain.

4. Put the roasted chillies and drained sun-dried tomatoes into a food processor with the garlic, oil, salt and chilli flakes and blend until smooth.

5. Transfer to an airtight container or a clean jar and keep in the fridge for up to 2 weeks.

LIST OF RECIPE PICTURES

Page numbers after each title are where you'll find the relevant recipe information.

ESSENTIALS AND EXTRAS

ACKNOWLEDGEMENTS

Thanks so much for making it this far! Although we are the authors of this book, it is the work of many more people who work behind the scenes, helping, supporting and inspiring us.

You would think that our fourth book would be easier, based on what we have learned from our previous books, but we have taken such a different approach it brought a new set of challenges.

First, thanks to our families for supporting, inspiring and always making our lives richer. Thanks to Justyna, May, Theo and Ned; Sabrina, Elsie, Issy and Janet (picture on the previous pages shows, *left to right*, May, Elsie, Issy, Ned and Theo). Special thanks to our Mom and Dad, Donal and Ismay, for without you both none of this would be possible – thanks for the constant encouragement and inspiration and for always being there when we need support. Dad, thanks for taking the mantle of the Happy Pear over the last number of years and for bearing with us always. Mom, thanks for caring so much and for always doing the less glamorous but vital jobs. To Darragh, our brother, who is an unsung hero of our story – for being the engine in the HP operation and as much a part of this story as we are, but rarely appearing in the limelight. We are very lucky to be your bro. To our other brother Mark for your help and support – it's great to have you back home so we can see more of you! And thanks to our sister-in-law, Yesim, for being so caring, considerate and always going above and beyond.

Thanks to Naomi Dooge (*pictured right*) for being the first member of our new food team. Naomi has been with us for eight years and has an amazing background as a chef – having trained at the legendary Ballymaloe Cookery School and the iconic American restaurant Chez Panisse, in Berkeley, California, and having also worked in a Boston institution, the Middle Eastern restaurant Oleana. Her vegan cooking journey started with us and she is an amazing recipe developer – tirelessly trialling recipes and being full of ideas, energy and patience. Thanks, Naomi, for being so wonderful to work with – for being so good at what you do; for being so professional; for putting up with our somewhat chaotic approach to work; and for being such a good and wise friend.

Thanks to some of the great chefs in our lives who have helped shape us and our views on food. Thanks to our 'chef mom', Dorene Palmer, and to Claire McCormack for being one of the best chefs we have worked with. Thanks to Paul Buggle and Noel Healy for being great chefs and such fun to work with.

Thanks to Charlotte O'Connell for all your wonderful work styling the photographs and working on the book shoot – you were a joy to work with. And thanks to Alistair Richardson for doing such a wonderful job. It's been great over the years working together to develop a friendship with you, Al, and really see you blossom into an incredible photographer.

Thanks to Abi Hartshorne for your fantastic work in figuring out the jigsaw of this book and creating such a strong design. Thanks also to Gail Jones and Viki Ottewill for your wonderful finishing touches on the design. Huge thanks to Richard Bravery and David Ettridge in the Penguin General Art Department for your ongoing help in bringing this big beast of a book to fruition! And a very special shout-out to the late and much loved Penguin art director, John Hamilton, for his belief in us and his incredible support to us over the years. We will always have a special place for you in our hearts, John.

Thanks to Kristen Jensen for editing a sprawling and complicated text with such intelligence and understanding. And thanks to Annie Lee for your top-class copy-editing – you are a pleasure to work with as always and have an amazing eye for detail.

Thanks to our agents, Faith O'Grady and Eavan Kenny of Lisa Richards – you guys are brill and a pleasure to work with.

At Penguin, thanks to our wonderful editor, Patricia Deevy, for putting your heart and soul into this project as always. You are amazing and we love you dearly! Thanks for all your support and guidance and your incredible work ethic – you rock! Thanks to Michael McLoughlin for being so solid and fair and wise to work with, and to the fantastic team in Penguin Ireland, especially Cliona Lewis, Louise Farrell and Aislin Reddie in publicity, Carrie Anderson and Brian Walker in sales, and Orla King in editorial. In London, thanks to Joanna Prior for your support and always being so lovely to deal with. Thanks to the magnificent Sam Fanaken in sales for your boundless enthusiasm and incredible focus. Also in London, thanks to Annie Underwood and Emma Brown – both of whom have guided the production journey of the book and made sure it arrived in your hands looking as well as it does. In comms, thanks to Amelia Fairney, Anna Ridley, Georgia Taylor, Rose Poole, Olivia Meade and Hannah Sawyer, who work so hard getting the word out in the UK. Thanks to Vanessa Forbes in rights, who has been talking it up a storm to publishers around the world. And thanks to Keeley Hughes, who makes sure that everything adds up!

Thanks to Niall Meehan. As well as being such a wonderful friend, for helping with some of the design, fonts and layout. Thanks to Ewelina Woo for your top-class creative ideas and input into the cover of the book. Thanks to Gerlinde Halmer for being so cool to work with and for all the great designs. Thanks to our cousin, the great Alan Kavanagh, for your advice on the cover design. Thanks for the dear friendship, Mark Lawlor and Damien Rice; we always value your opinions and company so much. Thanks for the inspiration and advice on this book.

Next, thanks to the fantastic team that makes the Happy Pear what it is. Without you there would be no Happy Pear.

Thanks to Seanie Cahill for the friendship. It's always wonderful to work with you. Thanks for the inspiration, constant support and for always being there. Thanks for being so patient with us and for doing such a good job with all our videos.

Thanks to Paul Murphy for being such a vital part of the HP story, for fitting in as though you were always a part of the team and for being so wise considering your young age! Thanks for putting up with us all.

Thanks to Jonny O'Donoghue for being the lord mayor of Pearville, for being so solid, responsible, straightforward and so good to work with. Thanks to the other vital members of our Pearville team, to Jennifer Rooney for being such a hard-working part of the HP for so long. Thanks to Gerard Flemming and Sean Willekens for all the wonderful NPD work you do, thanks to Joanna Glynn, Hannah Managan and Conor Kirwan for all your vital and caring HR work. Thanks to Anne Crotty for always being all over things, to Lorraine Clear for being so creative, and to Al Keighery for being a laugh and a techie hero. Thanks to Dee Cox, the queen of pesto, Will, the prince of pesto, and to all the wonderful and so hard-working pesto team: Steve, Apple, Brendan, Justyna, Magda, Alan, Justinas, and of course St Brendan (we will get to the mushrooms!).

Thanks to Fiona McBennett for always being so on the ball and for helping build and manage our online course with so much love and attention – you're fab, Fi! Thanks to the rest of our brilliant EME team, Elaine Kelly, the queen of online sales, with Ciara Hamilton, our social media ninja. Thanks to Ailish Doyle for help with social media.

Thanks to Joellen Jordan for always looking after us so well and for organizing so much of our life. Thanks for your support and for all the good laughs. Thanks to Paul Grimes and Shane Murphy, the coffee maestros – you are both legends, such a joy to work with and wonderful men. Paulie G, the chief, you're a true gentleman! Thanks to the legends that are Denis and Kris – Denis, you're one inspiring man, and Kris, you're a gent to work with. Thanks to Gerry for being with us so long and for always being so upbeat. Thanks to the rest of our sales team – Sandis and Cousin Paul – you are fab; thanks for all your mighty work, Chris Peare, Avril for being so hardworking, and welcome to the team, Will. Thanks to Cliodhna for being a top-class Yogi and promoter and to Brian for being so solid and nice to work alongside.

Thanks to our Shoreline team, led by Lisa and Eamhan, Joanna, Natasha, Kaitlin, Alex, Aisling; our production team of Terence, Netty, Victor, Paloma, Alana, Laila, Jack, Nathan, Margot, Szalos, Jutatip; our fabulous accounts department, led by Sharon, Jane, Evan and Katie; our world-class farmers, headed up by Steve, Tomek, Niamh and Lee; our stock and inventory team, led by the mighty Wayne – thanks for always being so up for it and positive: Dzieki, Michal, Stephen (L) and Stephen (H), Nathan (the best garda-to-be in the world!).

Thanks to Sorin Kiss and Charlie May for taking on great leadership in Church Road these days. Thanks to our Church Road team for always going above and beyond: Barry, Henrique, Marty, Polly, Jade, Jenna, Iqbal, Nora, Kitty, Sabrina, Ewelina, Kilian, Andrea, Kim, Sophia, Marlon, Kristel, our wonderful god-daughter Mia Smylle, Josh, Akos, Blue, Kevin, Hi Qiang. Thanks to Jen and Ross for looking after the veg shop so beautifully.

Thanks to Niamh Ahern, Dave McFadden and Paula Ruttle for all your hard work on quality control. Thanks to Aine Lynam for being so strong and such a good leader, you really are exceptional and so cool to work with. Thanks to our Clondalkin team, led by the great Marko and Filipe: Louise, Mary, Nicole, Anthony, Sam, Honora, Naoise, Alice, Zakir, John, Gyorgy and Gavin.

Thanks to our wonderful cousin Naomi Smith, we can't wait to have you back!

Thanks to all the Happy Pear team that have come and gone over the years – you have all had an impact on what the Happy Pear has become.

Thanks to our wonderful training and swim-rise crew, you enrich our lives in so many ways.

Finally, thanks to the people of our home town of Greystones and our extended community – thank you for your support, without it there would be no Happy Pear!

Dave & Steve x

INDEX

PENGUIN LIFE

UK | USA | Canada | Ireland | Australia
India | New Zealand | South Africa

Penguin Life is part of the Penguin Random House group of companies
whose addresses can be found at global.penguinrandomhouse.com.

First published 2020
002

Text copyright © David and Stephen Flynn, 2020
Photography copyright © Alistair Richardson, 2020

Designed by Hart Studio with additional work by Gail Jones and Viki Ottewill
Colour reproduction by Altaimage Ltd
Printed and bound in Italy by Printer Trento S.r.l.

A CIP catalogue record for this book is available from the British Library

ISBN: 978–1–844–88487–2

www.greenpenguin.co.uk

Penguin Random House is committed to a
sustainable future for our business, our readers
and our planet. This book is made from Forest
Stewardship Council® certified paper.